WORDS·TO·LIVE·BY

Twelve MONTHS OF DAYS

Daily Inspiration For

Twelve Step People

& Other Seekers

DAVID RIOUX

CompCare®Publishers

2415 ANNAPOLIS LANE
MINNEAPOLIS, MINNESOTA 55441

ISBN 0-89638-195-1
Cover & interior design by Lillian Svec

Inquiries, orders, and catalog requests
should be addressed to
CompCare Publishers
2415 Annapolis Lane
Minneapolis, Minnesota 55441
Call toll free 800/328-3330
(Minnesota residents 612/559-4800)

6   5   4   3   2   1
95 94 93 92 91 90

How joyful to look upon the awakened
And to keep company with the wise.
    —*The Buddha*

What the moment requires
the moment will provide.
    —*Goethe*

You shall be free indeed when your days
are not without a care nor your nights
without a want and a grief,
but rather when these things girdle your life
and yet you rise above them
naked and unbound.
    —*Kahlil Gibran*

ACKNOWLEDGMENTS

In giving birth to this book, the author
acknowledges the assistance and inspiration
provided by the following:
—my Higher Power
—my soulmate, Dianne
—Arthur and Rose
—Gabrielle
—Nicole
—Mary
—numerous professional colleagues
—friends from a number of Twelve Step Programs
—Father Sawyer, who encouraged me to write
—my editors, Kathy Garrett and Bonnie Hesse

1. We admitted we were powerless over alcohol — that our lives had become unmanageable.
2. Came to believe that a Power greater than ourselves could restore us to sanity.
3. Make a decision to turn our will and our lives over to the care of God *as we understood Him.*
4. Made a searching and fearless moral inventory of ourselves.
5. Admitted to God, to ourselves, and to another human being the exact nature of our wrongs.
6. Were entirely ready to have God remove these defects of character.
7. Humbly asked Him to remove our shortcomings.
8. Made a list of all persons we had harmed, and became willing to make amends to them all.
9. Made direct amends to such people wherever possible, except when to do so would injure them or others.
10. Continued to take personal inventory, and when we were wrong promptly admitted it.
11. Sought through prayer and meditation to improve our conscious contact with God *as we understood Him,* praying only for knowledge of His will for us and the power to carry that out.
12. Having had a spiritual awakening as the result of these steps, we tried to carry the message to other alcoholics and to practice these principles in all our affairs.

AA's Twelve Steps and the adapted Twelve Steps (opposite page) are printed with permission of AA World Services, Inc. Use of this material does not imply any affiliation with nor endorsement of this book by AA.

──── TWELVE STEPS FOR A PROGRAM OF PERSONAL DEVELOPMENT

1. We admitted that we were powerless and that our lives had become unmanageable.

2. Came to believe that a Power greater than ourselves could restore us to sanity.

3. Made a decision to turn our will and our lives over to the care of God as we understood the Divinity.

4. Made a searching and fearless moral inventory of ourselves.

5. Admitted to God, to ourselves, and to another human being the exact nature of our wrongs.

6. Were entirely ready to have God remove all these defects of character.

7. Humbly asked God to remove our shortcomings.

8. Made a list of all persons we had harmed, and became willing to make amends to them all.

9. Made direct amends to such people wherever possible, except when to do so would injure them or others.

10. Continued to take personal inventory and when we were wrong promptly admitted it.

11. Sought through prayer and meditation to improve our conscious contact with God as we understood the Divinity, praying only for knowledge of the divine will for us and the power to carry that out.

12. Having had a spiritual awakening as the result of these Steps, we tried to carry this message to others, and to practice these principles in all our affairs.

Twelve Step Thought

I can readily admit that I am powerless over my feelings and that my life has become unmanageable. I can't seem to control people around me. I can't even control my own internal reactions. Even so, I usually persist in relying on my ego and my self-will. In contrast, the teachings of the great sages echo the need to lose oneself, to let go. Maybe my New Year's resolution could focus on letting go of *my* way.

Sayings of the Sages

If any one would come after me, he must deny himself and take up his cross daily and follow me.
    —*Luke 9:23*

He who abandons all desires and acts free from longing, without any sense of mineness or egotism, he attains to peace.
    —*Bhagavad Gita II, 71*

A Hunk of Healing Humor

Humor is the miracle drug with no bad side effects.
    —*Lawrence J. Peter*

Daily Affirmation

I surrender *my* way, and I'm filled with relief.

Twelve Step Thought

Surrender is better than being a slave to my compulsions. This is not the capitulation of cowards. This is being in tune with the flow of what is. This is my reality. For me, ego and self-will have already proven inadequate, powerless. I choose to relieve myself of this terrible and unnecessary burden. My reliance will need to find another source of strength, a "higher" power. Paradoxically, admitting defeat is declaring freedom.

Sayings of the Sages

The man who loves his life will lose it, while the man who hates his life in this world will keep it for eternal life.
   —*John 12:25*

Contemplate much less the "I shall progress," than the "I" stand in "my way."
   —*Idries Shah, Reflections*

A Hunk of Healing Humor

You can't fall out of bed if you sleep on the floor.
   —*Herbert Prochnow*

Daily Affirmation

Today, I accept each moment as it is.

Twelve Step Thought

Today I realize that all my actions have consequences or "fruits." In the past, my petty personal power produced some really rotten fruits: obsessions, compulsions, impulsive behaviors. My vision was tricked by a facsimile of true Power, an ego fabrication. I experienced the ancient saying: as you sow, so shall you reap. The seeds I sowed were self-centeredness, flight from frustrations, conceit, and perfectionism. The crop that I reaped was fear, feelings of inadequacy, anger, self-indulgence. Then, several years of working Twelve Step Programs intervened. Now, I can plant grains that are bursting with love and peace.

Sayings of the Sages

The orchard where the tree grows is judged on the quality of its fruit, similarly a man's words betray what he feels.
—*Ecclesiastes 27:6*

Do you think you can take over the universe and improve it?
—*Tao Te Ching, 29*

A Hunk of Healing Humor

Adversity is the only diet that will reduce a fat head.
—*Jacob Braude*

Daily Affirmation

I accept my powerlessness and seek a Higher Power.

Twelve Step Thought

At the turning point in my sickness, I despised the sordid state of my spirit. I was sinking well below the level of powerlessness and unmanageability. Psychic pain pounded in me beyond all belief. Mental monsters were slowly sucking out the marrow of my soul. The groan in my gut grew deafening. Death would have provided soothing relief. But the plague that burned in my belly also infected my trigger finger. Finally, I just gave up and crumpled, sobbing "help" uncontrollably. And, in that time of complete surrender, an anonymous fellow lifted me up and struck a spark of hope.

Sayings of the Sages

Worn out with calling, my throat is hoarse, my eyes are strained, looking for my God.
—*Psalm 69:3*

Follow [the way] to the end of sorrow.
—*Dhammapada, 20*

A Hunk of Healing Humor

Agitation is the atmosphere of the brains.
—*Wendell Phillips*

Daily Affirmation

Today I am strengthened by spiritual fellowship.

Twelve Step Thought

For a long time, I didn't believe that I had a problem. After all, wasn't I dedicated to seeking the meaning of life? Any difficulties affecting me had to be due to the interference of others. Yet, I remember having worshipped faithfully before the altar of obsession. How irrational! While mocking those bound by boring routines, I consistently carried out sick, compulsive rituals. When I finally had hurt enough, I considered abandoning this base-metal idol and finding a golden god. In fact, at my moment of surrender, I was ready to do almost anything to have this terrible burden lifted from me.

Sayings of the Sages

That which is imperfect . . . would become tasteless and be as nothing to us.
—*Theologia Germanica, VI*

Without desire there is tranquility.
—*Tao Te Ching, 37*

A Hunk of Healing Humor

We ought never to do wrong when people are looking.
—*Mark Twain*

Daily Affirmation

A Higher Power has removed my burden.

Twelve Step Thought

When the anguish of my mental/emotional/physical illness grew great enough, I finally became willing to change. Before that, I kept postponing my getting better and kept believing that I could learn to control my problem. I let my ego distract me as I sank ever deeper into the quicksand of obsession. One day, the insanity of my condition was revealed to me in a flash. Then, I admitted personal powerlessness over my obsessive-compulsive traits. Now, for my life to be okay, I need to seek the comforting company of peers in mutual-support, self-help groups.

Sayings of the Sages

They shared everything they had.
  —*Acts 4:32*

Follow the awakened and set yourself free.
  —*Dhammapada, 5*

A Hunk of Healing Humor

If you suffer, thank God! It is a sure sign that you are alive.
  —*Elbert Hubbard*

Daily Affirmation

Relating to my support group comforts me today.

Twelve Step Thought

Step One implies recognizing my impulsive side too. "Impulsiveness" here means slipping into swift action without deliberation or aware determination. Many forces encourage me to succumb to the spur-of-the-moment, as if my physical and emotional needs can be satisfied by just the right "impulse buy." Additionally, my indeliberateness stems from perverted spontaneity, false pride, and reaction to self-perceived inadequacy. I feel healthier when I simply slow my lifepace, or when I only observe impulse-energy without responding. I try to think twice before acting; then, unhesitantly, I go for it.

Sayings of the Sages

For perceiving the meaning of . . . the sayings of the sages, let the wise listen and he will learn yet more.
　　　—Proverbs 1:5 & 6

Wakefulness is the way to life.
　　　—Dhammapada, 2

A Hunk of Healing Humor

I can resist anything except temptation.
　　　—Oscar Wilde

Daily Affirmation

Today I am thinking twice before acting.

Twelve Step Thought

My admission of powerlessness and unmanageability saw me soar to greater heights. This spiritual trip seems like a spiral winding upward. At each spin of the spiral, I reach a new plateau of personal development. Stepping onto that plateau requires a redoing of Step One. Yet, it's not really a repetition, because the whole world metamorphoses again at the top of each turn. So "redoing" becomes doing anew. Miraculously, my spirit is shot through a space/time warp to the doorway of a whole new dimension.

Sayings of the Sages

In this path, no effort is ever lost and no obstacle prevails.
— *Bhagavad Gita II, 40*

Man does not have a capacity of instant comprehension.
— *Idries Shah, Reflections*

A Hunk of Healing Humor

"Be yourself!" is about the worse advice you can give to some people.
— *John Masefield*

Daily Affirmation

I am being transported to ever higher dimensions.

Twelve Step Thought

Upon making daily meditation the cornerstone of my spiritual growth program, my whole attitude and outlook on life began to change. Gradually my doing meditation became meditation doing me. Quite a positive reinforcement of personal powerlessness! The process reminds me of an ancient gnostic lesson, relating that the soul has two eyes. The right eye sees into eternity; the left eye, into time and temporal things. In the enlightened person, both eyes view together. For me and for most of us, it's one eye at a time. The purpose of daily quiet time is to strengthen the vision of Oneness.

Sayings of the Sages

If therefore your eye is good, your whole body will be full of light.
    —*Matthew 6:22*

If the soul shall see with the right eye into eternity, then the left eye must close itself and refrain from working.
    —*Theologia Germanica, VII*

A Hunk of Healing Humor

You are only what you are when no one is looking.
    —*Robert C. Edwards*

Daily Affirmation

The quiet of meditation is filtering into my day.

Twelve Step Thought

For a long time, I felt it just wasn't fair that I got so many bad breaks. I sought the highest values, yet ended up in the lowest places. It seemed like I tried my best; nevertheless, I was constantly beaten back by my own character flaws. Adding insult to injury, I was advised to admit lack of control and power. Then, I learned that accepting the way things are constitutes the first step in changing my life for the better. "Fairness" implies expectations of what *should* be. Inner worth doesn't depend on outer conditions. And I can't always expect to be happy about outcomes in this world. But then, whoever said life is fair?

Sayings of the Sages

Even the man of knowledge acts in accordance with his own nature.
　　—Bhagavad Gita III, 33

See the world as it is, and death shall overlook you.
　　—Dhammapada, 13

A Hunk of Healing Humor

Truth is beautiful, without doubt; but so are lies.
　　—Ralph Waldo Emerson

Daily Affirmation

I accept and love myself as I am.

Twelve Step Thought

In declaring that I was without strength and that my back was to the wall, I avowed, in a sense, my own extinction. Like the proverbial peeled onion, a thick layer of my ego had to be stripped away and discarded for me to admit defeat. Knowing that I was stepping up to my demise, I approached this "peeling" only after a lot of kicking and screaming. Finally, harboring a spark of hope deep in my heartgut, I plunged into the dazzling darkness of dissolution. Surprise! I emerged into peaceful light. I was reborn. That little "death" led me to a much larger life.

Sayings of the Sages

For in the true life of Christ, the self and the me and nature must be forsaken and lost, and die altogether.
    —*Theologia Germanica, XX*

He is not here: he has risen, just as he said.
    —*Matthew 28:6*

Empty and be full; wear out and be new.
    —*Tao Te Ching, 22*

A Hunk of Healing Humor

Most people would rather die than think: many do.
    —*Bertrand Russell*

Daily Affirmation

Today I find joy in the fullness of life.

Twelve Step Thought

There was a time when I could not admit that I had any dependency problems. In order to function, I felt I needed acceptable crutches to lean on. In fact, I exchanged precarious independence for the supposed security of numerous dependencies. Afraid of facing painful reality and of possibly enduring the humiliation of being wrong, I opted for compulsive subservience to many masters: day-dreams, novels, sex, relationships, alcohol, cigarettes, drugs, food, buying sprees. As my bondage became unbearable, I sought relief in the paradox of powerlessness and in a self-help program of recovery. Eventually, I gained freedom via a process imbued with ever-growing responsibility for being me.

Sayings of the Sages

No one can serve two masters.
   —*Matthew 6:24*

Do thy work, . . . abandoning attachment.
   —*Bhagavad Gita II, 48*

A Hunk of Healing Humor

One advantage in being stupid is that you never get lonely.
   —*Herbert Prochnow*

Daily Affirmation

I am tuned in to being responsible and free.

Twelve Step Thought

At one time, most meaning in my life was derived from helping persons "weaker" than I. Living on the surface of my personality, there I safely touched others. Plenty of people-pleasing, with little space for profoundly pleasing me, although there were some extreme attempts at self-gratification. Mostly, I found pitiful pleasure in rescuing/fixing so-and-so. When I even noticed me, I felt an eerie emptiness rolling around in my gut. After years of denial, my unhappiness could no longer be ignored. And—thanks to the support of Twelve Step groups, meditation, prayer—I let go of *you* to finally take hold of *me*.

Sayings of the Sages

To straighten the crooked you must first . . . straighten yourself.
        —*Dhammapada, 12*

You have delivered me from the strivings of the people.
        —*Psalm 18:43*

A Hunk of Healing Humor

Pity the meek, for they shall inherit the earth.
        —*Don Marquis*

Daily Affirmation

I best help others by improving myself.

Twelve Step Thought

I can best describe my chronic condition as a mixture of excessive self-focus and real need to serve. When others were looking, I portrayed altruism; when alone, I wallowed in self-absorption—both as overindulgence and guilt. Despite low self-esteem, I constantly struggled to achieve balance. I often exhibited defensive behavior or sudden anger in response to criticism. How dare anyone question my adequacy? At last, this route proved too painful to follow. Luckily, others who had left this path were willing to share their experiences. I now trust my H.P. will show me the way.

Sayings of the Sages

The ten thousand things rise and fall without cease: Creating, yet not possessing; working, yet not taking credit.

 —*Tao Te Ching, 2*

He seeketh alone the honour of God, and not his own.
 —*Theologia Germanica, X*

A Hunk of Healing Humor

Some people have tact; others tell the truth.
 —*Jacob Braude*

Daily Affirmation

Today my Higher Power is the center of my life.

Twelve Step Thought

I kept assuming the unnecessary burden of justifying my actions. A special friend of mine frequently advised: "Don't explain. Don't defend." Why feel defensive about someone else's comments? Others' remarks are just a reflection of them, their perceptions and their attitudes. Anyway, no mere verbiage will affect me unless I allow it to. Deep truth can be found in the seemingly trite children's adage: "Sticks and stones may break my bones, but names will never hurt me." When someone appears to be berating me, I can concentrate silently on sending love to that person.

Sayings of the Sages

When thy intelligence shall cross the turbidity of delusion, then shalt thou become indifferent to what has been heard.
    —*Bhagavad Gita II, 52*

Who is the wrong person to criticize? You.
    —*Idries Shah, Reflections*

A Hunk of Healing Humor

A critic is a legless person who teaches running.
    —*Channing Pollock*

Daily Affirmation

What others say belongs to them.

Twelve Step Thought

I found many ways to deny the seriousness of my condition. Projection (placing my guilt in another individual) was a favorite: "Just look how X hurts others by being so selfish!" Minimization (declaring the disaster isn't that bad) was another: "Gee, most of the time I get by okay. I only go off the deep end twice a year." Repression (stuffing the monster in my unconscious mind) was a frequent escape: "What problem? I'm a happy-go-lucky person." Persecution (blaming others for my problems) was a recurring dodge: "See what they're doing to me! No wonder I'm so messed up." One day, I ran out of excuses. Unbearable pain mirrored the reality of my sickness. In desperation, I sought help.

Sayings of the Sages

[Alone] I am not able to stand steady. My mind is reeling.
    —*Bhagavad Gita I, 30*

See the false as false, the true as true.
    —*Dhammapada, 1*

A Hunk of Healing Humor

When I am angry at myself, I criticize others.
    —*Ed Howe*

Daily Affirmation

Look for the truth, and look out for denial.

Twelve Step Thought

One of the greatest obstacles to my recovery was the mental image of myself as a victim. I knew that I had gotten well before; but, then, I became sick again. The tricky question was: How could I *remain* better? Clearly I suffered from an obsession so subtle, so powerful that my best will power crumbled before it. How can anyone weather a cyclone in a rowboat? Unbelievably, I was told the solution is to throw away the oars! Even confronted with this paradoxical truth, I desperately longed to be like the phoenix—that mystical bird reborn from the ashes of its own annihilation. Instead, I traded rowing frantically for flowing with the current.

Sayings of the Sages

Nothing is complained of, save only what is contrary to God.
    —*Theologia Germanica, LI*

The world is ruled by letting things take their course.
    —*Tao Te Ching, 48*

A Hunk of Healing Humor

Cheer up, the worst is yet to come.
    —*Philander Johnson*

Daily Affirmation

Today I am going with the flow.

Twelve Step Thought

By my grandiose gestures, I spread self-centeredness before the populace to distract it (and me) from self-perceived, cringing inadequacy. To maintain this fiction, I *needed* to impress others. And God forbid that a mistake should be made—especially *in front of people*! So grandiosity, trying to seem very important, made me adopt an all-or-nothing approach to coping with life's situations. I suffered a double whammy: the self-abasing pangs of unworthiness, and the overreactions of brassy egomania. Then, I began leaving the pompous and showy behind, and accepting me as okay. Now I'm learning to enjoy pausing and being still.

Sayings of the Sages

The true man of old . . . stood straight and firm and did not waver. He was of humble mien but was not servile.
　　—*Chuang Tsu: Inner Chapters, 6*

When the mind runs after roving senses, it carries away understanding.
　　—*Bhagavad Gita II, 67*

A Hunk of Healing Humor

The best way to get praise is to die.
　　—*Italian proverb*

Daily Affirmation

My understanding is anchored in the quiet of my inner self.

Twelve Step Thought

Undoubtedly, I was among the majority that would not work a Twelve Step Program or any serious personal discipline unless "bottom" was reached. By this, I mean experiencing an emotional low so painful that death (of spirit) seemed imminent. Yet, my moment of supreme crisis became the jumping-off point from which sprang a positive restructuring of my whole life. The discomfort of working through my bottom seemed not so bad compared to the horrible hurt of hiding in mental illness and of clutching a self-destructive mindset. Looking back, I see the fearful unknown evaporating like mist; I remember pivotal days with joyful tears.

Sayings of the Sages

I am the man who obscured Your designs with my empty-headed words.
        —*Job 42:3*

Remove your own impurities little by little.
        —*Dhammapada, 18*

A Hunk of Healing Humor

When you are getting kicked from the rear it means you're in front.
        —*Bishop Fulton Sheen*

Daily Affirmation

Today I am leaving another fear behind me.

Twelve Step Thought

Before I found solid meaning in my life, I trudged through the desert of an inner barren state, a sort of existential wasteland. In character, I tried to fill a perceived "hole" in my being. I forced harmful objects (drugs, selfish sex, sick eating habits, other obsessions) into an ever-emptier lifespace. I felt like a vacant lot. It was only when I totally emptied myself that a purposeful solidity began to form within my surrender. Welcome warmth seeped in from newfound friends who had overcome a like experience. Now, my space fills increasingly with love of living beyond myself.

Sayings of the Sages

For those in whom ignorance is destroyed by wisdom, for them wisdom lights up the Supreme Self like the sun.
　　　—Bhagavad Gita V, 16

The Tao is an empty vessel; it is used, but never filled.
　　　—Tao Te Ching, 4

A Hunk of Healing Humor

It is a sin to believe evil of others, but it is seldom a mistake.
　　　—H. L. Mencken

Daily Affirmation

My attention is on the meaning in my life.

Twelve Step Thought

Yesterday, I was stuck in my obsessions and failures. Then, the logjam was broken for me. Today, part of my progress consists in remembering where I came from. In some Twelve Step Programs, such recall is titled "keeping your memory green." It doesn't mean dwelling morbidly on prior psychological/physical trauma. Remembrance is a prod to moving along in a spiritual growth process. Otherwise, I will wallow in some miserable mental state rather than flowing with the moment. The periodic review of where I started from reinforces in me that I have come quite far and that I am supported by a Force much greater than my poor personality.

Sayings of the Sages

When I am in trouble, you come to my relief.
    —*Psalm 4:1*

It is God who works in you to will and do what pleases him.
    —*Philippians 2:13*

A Hunk of Healing Humor

Experience: A comb life gives you after you lose your hair.
    —*Judith Stern*

Daily Affirmation

Remembering where I started gives me gratitude for where I am.

Twelve Step Thought

At some point, I acquired a fixation on avoiding wrongness. A strange defensiveness developed in me—waxing and waning like the tides generated by an emotional moon. Maybe I'm living with a curse carried over from other lifetimes. And this brainwashing bases my personal worth on the opinion of others. They *must* like me—at any cost. Eventually, this led me to walk around with a paranoid chip on my shoulder. Before a constructive thought can form and direct me, this warped "protective" trait overwhelms me. Then I lash out, and hurt someone. For now, my best is apologizing to the injured party. For later, I pray this defect will be removed.

Sayings of the Sages

What I want to do I do not, but what I hate to do.
    —*Romans 7:15*

Men do not forget what ought to be forgotten, but forget what ought not to be forgotten.
    —*Chuang Tsu: Inner Chapters, 5*

A Hunk of Healing Humor

To his dog, every man is Napoleon; hence the constant popularity of dogs.
    —*Aldous Huxley*

Daily Affirmation

My Higher Power is removing my fixation on avoiding wrongness.

Twelve Step Thought

Lately, I sometimes even look for the point of discomfort so that I might pass through it, experiencing a spurt of growth. Yet, for many years, I carefully avoided any situation that might be uncomfortable. My denying behavior accumulated guilt pangs and feelings of inadequacy. Avoiding pain became a goal, instead of a means, for living. Whoever presented me with a seemingly unpleasant communication was picking on me, criticizing me, accusing me of being incompetent. Some paranoid viewpoint! Today, I realize that feeling uncomfortable can be a springboard to greater peace of mind.

Sayings of the Sages

Blessed are those who wash their robes, that they may have the right to the tree of life.
        —*Revelation 22:14*

In this Paradise [this world], all things are lawful, save one tree and the fruits thereof. Of all things there are . . . nothing is contrary to God but one thing only: that is, self-will.
        —*Theologia Germanica, L*

A Hunk of Healing Humor

I have great faith in fools—self-confidence my friends call it.
        —*Edgar Allen Poe*

Daily Affirmation

Feeling uncomfortable will remind me to seek God's will.

Twelve Step Thought

When I remember, I know who I really am. In those moments, I see the powerlessness of my "little" self. Once more, I transcend my limited ego to reach the Greater Self, the highest power. When I am more often aware of this Presence, deep peace prevails. Yet, I frequently get stuck in my surface consciousness. I choose sleep instead of awakeness. I am opening gradually to the pure Awareness, a sort of witness state beyond my mind. When I do recall, I feel in balance. On one level, it's okay to admit character faults; on a deeper level, I touch an incredible strength that powers the upliftment of my spirit.

Sayings of the Sages

You have not forgotten to remember; you have remembered to forget. But people can forget to forget.
    —*Idries Shah, Reflections*

Oh, hidden deep but ever present!
    —*Tao Te Ching, 4*

A Hunk of Healing Humor

You must believe in God, in spite of what the clergy say.
    —*Benjamin Jowett*

Daily Affirmation

Today, I'm in touch with my Greater Self.

Twelve Step Thought

Ever since I can remember, I was bothered by a sense of inadequacy. Whatever prompted my low self-esteem remains unknown. I do know that, to avoid the pain of feeling less-than, I acted as if everything were fine in my life. I hid my real self behind an air of innocence and a silver tongue. My relationships were mostly shallow. With my negative outlook, I ignored some possible and quite interesting life goals. Tired of the troubles brought on by my bad attitude, I finally sought help. A Power greater than myself graced me with relief and a healthier way to live. Now, I feel good about me and share myself more honestly.

Sayings of the Sages

We are what we think.
    —*Dhammapada, 1*

The Lord takes pleasure in those who fear Him.
    —*Psalm 147:11*

A Hunk of Healing Humor

If God wanted us to be brave, why did he give us legs?
    —*Marvin Kitman*

Daily Affirmation

My Higher Power makes me 100 percent adequate.

Twelve Step Thought

For me, "egocentric" means selfishness in its most negative sense. My ego focus consisted of mind tripping, characterized by being dishonest about how I felt. So wrapped up was I in denying feelings that my blindsidedness almost ended my life. I ignored the affective aspects of others, not wanting to face my own emotionality. Sharing my inner impressions with *anyone* was very difficult. Now, I perceive that I'm not a solitary star with all others as planets. I've come to know that I circle, and am warmed by, the same sun as everyone else. And I'm becoming more open, willing to share.

Sayings of the Sages

God is flawless and the same in all.
    —*Bhagavad Gita V, 19*

When the wind blows through the ten thousand hollows, they all make their own sounds. Why should there be anything else that causes the sound?
    —*Chuang Tsu: Inner Chapters, 2*

A Hunk of Healing Humor

Diplomacy is the knack of letting the other fellow have *your* way.
    —*Abraham Lincoln*

Daily Affirmation

Today I celebrate my greater openness with others.

Twelve Step Thought

An ego aspect that caused me much agony is referred to by some Twelve Step Programs as "self-will run riot." In my scenario, the world is a play; and I am the director. And *I* expect to determine the conclusion of each act. Also, I anticipate that all actors will follow *my* directions. In contrast, I found myself wrapped in unrealistic expectations and uncontrollable outcomes. Crazily, I believed my own storyline: if I tried hard enough, I would gain my fondest wishes. Then, a moment of revelation made my assumptions seem assinine. Lately, I'm learning to accept life on life's terms.

Sayings of the Sages

All he says tends to mischief and deceit, he has turned his back on wisdom.
  —*Psalm 36:3*

He who knows when to stop does not find himself in trouble.
  —*Tao Te Ching, 44*

A Hunk of Healing Humor

If what you don't know can't hurt you, some persons are hurtproof.
  —*Anonymous*

Daily Affirmation

I'm letting a Higher Power direct the play today.

Twelve Step Thought

Seeking spiritual growth means accepting changes in my life. Such basic alterations require the restructuring of ego, breaking apart my old identity so a new model can be assembled. Ouch! This causes me fear and anguish. For me, growing means wanting to grow more than wanting to avoid the painfulness involved. In other words, no pain, no gain. So, for me and my fellow seekers, change is characterized by a large amount of discomfort. Spirituality is not mouthing pious platitudes. It's facing the monsters released by my unconscious and surviving their bloody departure.

Sayings of the Sages

The heart of the wise is in the house of mourning, the heart of fools in the house of mirth.
    —*Ecclesiastes 7:4*

We make to ourselves much disquietude and difficulty which we might well be spared and raised above.
    —*Theologia Germanica, XXI*

A Hunk of Healing Humor

Lots of folks confuse bad management with destiny.
    —*Kin Hubbard*

Daily Affirmation

I am willing to pay the price for spiritual growth.

Twelve Step Thought

Thinking concretely, I see responsibility as the ability to respond. Yet, I finally can admit I'm powerless over my moods and over my ideas. Feelings and thoughts flash through me; then, as quickly, they vanish. The crucial point is how I acknowledge these appearances in my consciousness. I determine how I reply to these emotional/mental stimuli. I can control my answering actions. I can practice desired responsiveness and set standards for action. Most of all, I can respond to others with love rather than fear. I seek to do what needs doing in unison with the Universal Flow.

Sayings of the Sages

For this we labor and strive, that we have put our hope in the living God, who is the Saviour of all men.
    —*I Timothy 4:10*

In all his actions the master discriminates, and he becomes pure.
    —*Dhammapada, 21*

A Hunk of Healing Humor

In going through the checkout lane of life, the person to watch is the person behind the person in front of you.
    —*Anonymous*

Daily Affirmation

Today I will respond lovingly to everyone I meet.

Twelve Step Thought

Having had my fill of hurt, I now recognize that selfish behavior leads only to short-term pleasure and long-term pain. So I stop grabbing selfishness and seek a dignified state. When I surrender, I secure dignity by accepting myself exactly as I am. To accept me, I must get to know me and my Higher Power. This is healthy pride, healthy humility, healthy self-esteem. Integrity established, at times I still will battle to preserve a feeling of uprightness. My goal: spiritual respectability, quiet bliss. I realize my fullest human potential by letting my light shine.

Sayings of the Sages

Mistaking the false for the true and the true for the false, you overlook the heart and fill yourself with desire.
    —Dhammapada, 1

No one lights a lamp and puts it in a place where it will be hidden.
    —Luke 11:33

A Hunk of Healing Humor

It is dangerous to be sincere unless you are also stupid.
    —George Bernard Shaw

Daily Affirmation

My human dignity is upheld by my Higher Power.

Twelve Step Thought

Over the past few years, I've come to understand and accept that life is basically a solitary journey. My mind constitutes a prison cell, though I seek others and join other seekers on a spiritual path. From solitary confinement, reaching out to fellows, my being is squeezed between the tight bars of mere words and gestures. There is no total communion in deepest joy. In fact, it's hard to find happiness in myself; never mind finding it elsewhere. Sages say we all share this dilemma. And there is consolation in keeping like-minded company. Paradoxically, I sense that all souls are totally united in the infinite aloneness of the Universal Mind.

Sayings of the Sages

In truth, All is One and One is All in God.
   —*Theologia Germanica, XLVI*

When there is no more separation between "this" and "that," it is called the still-point of Tao.
   —*Chuang Tsu: Inner Chapters, 2*

A Hunk of Healing Humor

There is no cure for birth or death save to enjoy the interval.
   —*George Santayana*

Daily Affirmation

Today I savor the alone stillness within me.

Twelve Step Thought

Yes, I have come to believe that a Power greater than my "self" is restoring my sense of balance. When I first became a Twelve Stepper, I gave mostly lip service to any such power. Selfishness strongly hinted that I alone was renovating me. However, frequent discordant notes in my gut, linked with spasmodic urges for growth, led me to truly accept a Higher Power. I remembered that, although "I" was powerless, a tyrannical obsession had been removed from my mind.

Sayings of the Sages

Yahweh, the king rejoices in your power; what great joy your saving help gives him!
    —*Psalm 21:1*

I am the way and the truth and the life.
    —*John 14:6*

A Hunk of Healing Humor

He who laughs, lasts.
    —*Mary Pettibone Poole*

Daily Affirmation

I am being renewed by my Higher Power.

Twelve Step Thought

Sometimes I catch myself acting insanely. For me, being insane is being off balance. When I'm physically off balance, I can fall and hurt myself. A similar crash happens when I'm hurting mentally and emotionally. All my head trips are pain-producing: worry, obsessive mindset, desire to control others, negative thinking. The word *sane* derives from the Latin *sanus*—meaning "sound," "whole," "healthy." When I focus on the Source of health, then I'm restored to being sound, whole, balanced.

Sayings of the Sages

What is this teaching? With authority and power, he gives orders to unclean spirits and they come out!
    —*Luke 4:36*

If one is sick of sickness, then one is not sick; the sage is not sick because he is sick of sickness.
    —*Tao Te Ching, 71*

A Hunk of Healing Humor

Only the mediocre are always at their best.
    —*Jean Giraudoux*

Daily Affirmation

Today, I'm centered and well balanced.

Twelve Step Thought

My chaotic paranoia included someone or something shadowing me, sneaking up on me. Of course, with danger coming from the rear, my back was exposed. I could only defend in the direction I could see. And I couldn't see directly behind myself. So I spent some time whirling around to see who/what might be there. Over more time, I grew to understand the insanity of maintaining a fearful world filled with nonexistent threats. Then, I came to believe that a Higher Power was watching over me. Now, I can breathe easier, knowing that my back is covered.

Sayings of the Sages

Of the non-existent there is no coming to be; of the existent there is no ceasing to be.
    —*Bhagavad Gita II, 16*

I take shelter in the shadow of your wings.
    —*Psalm 57:1*

A Hunk of Healing Humor

I am a kind of paranoiac in reverse. I suspect people of plotting to make me happy.
    —*J. D. Salinger*

Daily Affirmation

My Higher Power is watching over me.

Twelve Step Thought

On my recovery road, I experienced a slow but definite progression. First, I came. I dragged my benumbed body to Twelve Step meetings. I sought a source of strength. Then, I came to. I snapped out of my mental fog and into seeing the sorriness of my state, like someone had switched on the lightbulb of awareness. Finally, I came to believe—holding not just an intellectual credence but a living faith in a Power greater than myself. With the lamp of wisdom lighting the way, God guides my footsteps across time's path.

Sayings of the Sages

The Lord went before them . . . by night in a pillar of fire to give them light.
    —Exodus 13:21

In all matters, great or small, few will succeed without following Tao.
    —Chuang Tsu: Inner Chapters, 4

A Hunk of Healing Humor

God heals and the doctor takes the fee.
    —Benjamin Franklin

Daily Affirmation

Today, God is guiding my footsteps.

Twelve Step Thought

A Power greater than my limited ego definitely restored meaning to my life. Before that happened, I screamed obscenities silently at the people-parade around me. I despised the "what" of this world. "How" and "why" only confused me. Who can accept a single ancestor screwing all of us? Insane behavior and addictions were my way of parrying thrusts from the flaming sword guarding the Garden of Eden. Then, filled with desperate faith, I let go of my insanity; I placed total trust in an unknown loving Force. And I was graced with a new sense of purpose and of being loved.

Sayings of the Sages

Live in your heart.
        —*Dhammapada, 14*

A broken and contrite heart, O God, you will not despise.
        —*Psalm 51:17*

A Hunk of Healing Humor

The world is proof that God is a committee.
        —*Bob Stokes*

Daily Affirmation

I find the meaning of life deep in my heart.

Twelve Step Thought

After many a sad experience of seeking my own little
truth, I now believe that knowing Truth will free me
from all human bondage. A Power much greater than
myself will restore the original birthright, the divine
spark that spun out into darkness innumerable light
years ago. Or was it just yesterday . . .? What I do
know is this: I fear the dark; I rush to embrace the
light. When I'm immersed in lightful love, fearfulness
no longer exists. When the darkening obscures my
mind, I become the slave of a shadow world. Yet, in the
knowing lightfulness, I live peacefully—truly free from
fear.

Sayings of the Sages

Those that know me are few.
　　—*Tao Te Ching, 70*

You will know the truth, and the truth will set you free.
　　—*John 8:32*

A Hunk of Healing Humor

No one is perfect, but some idiots are getting close.
　　—*Anonymous*

Daily Affirmation

Today I am being led into the light.

Twelve Step Thought

A sense of balance and peace infiltrated my life as I turned ever more toward a strength greater than myself. Intuitively, I knew it was my spirit, my deepest inner self that does this turning. Reflected in the mirror of my mind's eye, a silent observer swings about. It moves without effort, yet with utmost exertion. I'm facing the featureless visage of the all-penetrating Presence. Simultaneously, ultimate excitement and supreme calm are experienced—perceived in some psychic view uncluttered by either time or space. In a split-second surge of bluebolt energy, even my nametag is wiped clean. Beyond coming to believe, I dissolve in Higher Power.

Sayings of the Sages

Whoever lives by the truth comes into the light.
—*John 3:21*

As soon as a man turneth himself in spirit, and with his whole heart and mind entereth into the mind of God which is above time, all that ever he hath lost is restored in a moment.
—*Theologia Germanica, VIII*

A Hunk of Healing Humor

Positive anything is better than negative nothing.
—*Elbert Hubbard*

Daily Affirmation

I believe my Higher Power restores me.

Twelve Step Thought

Left to my own devices, I constantly become the victim of addictive infirmities. My limited ego is not that reliable Power which elicits a healthy and sane response. A Spirit-Strength plucks me from the stormy seas of my obsessiveness, and returns me to harbor at my serene center. In the spiritness is a pattern that connects all for me—serving as a powerful and comforting backdrop to the play of being. And identification with spiritbeing is my restorative connection to this Higher Power.

Sayings of the Sages

You are here to kneel where prayer has been valid.
    —*T. S. Eliot, Little Gidding*

People used to play with toys. Now the toys play with them.
    —*Idries Shah, Reflections*

A Hunk of Healing Humor

God made everything out of nothing, but the nothingness shows through.
    —*Paul Valery*

Daily Affirmation

Spirit is my strength.

Twelve Step Thought

In the dark days before and during my addiction, I muddled through many manifestations of personal powerlessness. I slipped and slid in a mental mudhole of martyrdom and dependency. I really felt that, if I always pleased others, I would be safe. Maybe they wouldn't discover how inadequate and fearful I was. Feeling dry inside, I decided God had abandoned me. My sometimes salvation was chemically induced. So was my hell. Only much later in my play, when a Shining Strength restored me, did I discover that I truly am okay. My victim state was just a stage prop, illusory. For the gift of hope, I'm grateful today.

Sayings of the Sages

My body, too, abides in confidence; because you will not abandon my soul to the nether world.
  —*Psalm 16:9 & 10*

Set things in order before there is confusion.
  —*Tao Te Ching, 64*

A Hunk of Healing Humor

Luck: when bad fortune follows me, but never catches up.
  —*Anonymous*

Daily Affirmation

I'm grateful to my Higher Power for hope.

Twelve Step Thought

Restoration implies a state of being that once existed, was lost, and was brought back. I don't believe that I ever possessed any saneness. Before the cancerlike flowering of my addictions occurred, I experienced mostly the stinging sands of self-recrimination and inadequacy, blown about in the barren desert of my mind. I hardly knew the "high" called sanity. Yet, upon my admission of defeat, some Blessed Breath inflated the shrivelled balloon of my soul. Like T. S. Eliot, I am arriving where I started, and I am knowing the place for the first time.

Sayings of the Sages

By the grace of God, I am what I am.
   —*I Corinthians 15:10*

I think that the mind is as difficult to control as the wind.
   —*Bhagavad Gita VI, 34*

A Hunk of Healing Humor

Nothing is quite so annoying as to have someone go right on talking when you're interrupting.
   —*Herbert Prochnow*

Daily Affirmation

A Power greater than myself breathes for me.

Twelve Step Thought

One fine day, the meaning of humility dawned on me. Didn't I come into this world with empty hands? And, soon enough, I'll leave it just as I arrived: with empty hands. Whatever I have is a gift from a Source greater and better than myself. Even though evidence of mental ability had been well demonstrated prior to the insanity of my addiction, I had to realize that intellectual gifts were just that: gifts. For me, intellect and humility could be compatible—*if* I placed humility first.

Sayings of the Sages

This humility springeth up in the man, because in the true Light he seeth that Substance, Life, Perceiving, Knowledge, Power, and what is thereof, do all belong to the True Good, and not to the creature.
　　—Theologia Germanica, XXXV

Blessed are the poor in spirit.
　　—Matthew 5:3

A Hunk of Healing Humor

I was born modest; not all over, but in spots.
　　—Mark Twain

Daily Affirmation

Everything I have is a gift.

Twelve Step Thought

My addictive defiance and my human nature resist basic change wherever possible. Yet, I'm a changed person. Thus, I'm starting to understand that a special Power of spirit is doing for me now what I couldn't do for myself before. The long-term results of this super-human assistance are loving, joyous, peaceful, and gentle. Given such rewards, I have decided to pay whatever price in humility (at times feeling like "humil-iation") that is exacted of me. Any psychic pain involved is just part of the growing process. Growth equals change equals pain. And a mysterious Force is guiding me to a healthy state of mind.

Sayings of the Sages

The fruit of the Spirit is love, joy, peace, patience, kindness, goodness, faithfulness, gentleness and self-control.
—*Galatians 5:22 & 23*

A master is never proud.
—*Dhammapada, 26*

A Hunk of Healing Humor

Everything is funny as long as it is happening to somebody else.
—*Will Rogers*

Daily Affirmation

No pain, no gain.

Twelve Step Thought

Of the immense insanity of my life, there was absolutely no doubt. In many ways, I lived as if others existed only to meet my needs. At work, I was simultaneously fearful and daredevilish. Whenever I was criticized, I knew jealous "higher-ups" were trying to do me in. On the other hand, I took tremendous political risks that could have endangered companies for which I worked. At home, I managed to step on my own heart and those of family members. In my frantic pace, I ignored the age-old adage: *Festina lente* or, "Make haste slowly." Finally I came to believe that a powerful Spiritfriend could transform my crazy mind.

Sayings of the Sages

What is sometimes thought to be clever is, significantly often, merely an advanced form of foolishness.
　　—*Idries Shah, Reflections*

I have foolishly squandered my energy.
　　—*Chuang Tsu: Inner Chapters, 5*

A Hunk of Healing Humor

Life being what it is, one dreams of revenge.
　　—*Paul Gauguin*

Daily Affirmation

A powerful Friend is transforming my crazy mind.

Twelve Step Thought

Reliance (instead of *defiance*) now characterizes my belief in a better way. Previously, a defiant mood permeated my life. Feeling let down by a supposedly merciful deity, I defied this capricious creator as well as his creation. Deep down inside, I trusted nobody—least of all myself. Paradoxically, my low self-esteem generated ever-higher levels of defiance. Others reacted to my habit of defying with hurtful retaliation, so that I retreated further into my addiction. Then, after hitting my bottom, I started to seek some sanity and to rely on a Higher Power.

Sayings of the Sages

I have trust now and no fear.
    —Isaiah 12:2

Every good and perfect gift is from above, coming down from the Father of lights, who does not change like shifting shadows.
    —James 1:17

A Hunk of Healing Humor

Have you noticed now many people say, "I wasn't born yesterday," and act as if they were only born today?
    —Idries Shah, Reflections

Daily Affirmation

I can rely on my Higher Power.

Twelve Step Thought

My Twelve Step, mutual-support group recommends that I be open and keep an open mind. In truth, for many years, I was a closed corporation. How easily kindred spirits recognize the fixed and judgmental nature of my mind! And, yet, no specific belief ever is demanded of me. I'm reminded fairly often that any words of advice are suggestions based on the personal experience of prior members. Anyway, in doing what is recommended, I'm discovering gradually a Power greater than myself. I've found a method of personal growth that really works.

Sayings of the Sages

With an open mind, you will be openhearted. Being openhearted, you will act royally. Being royal, you will attain the divine.
　　—*Tao Te Ching, 16*

Thoroughly to know oneself . . . is the highest art.
　　—*Theologia Germanica, IX*

A Hunk of Healing Humor

Every day people are straying away from the church and going back to God.
　　—*Lenny Bruce*

Daily Affirmation

Today, I'm open-minded, and I'm really growing.

Twelve Step Thought

The *experience* of coming to believe happened as instant, intuitive knowing—suffused with calming energy—like being securely suspended in a giant cocoon and having my central core gently and soothingly rocked to and fro. This was no intellectual proposition. Rather, I inhaled the mind-blowing and timeless realization that I was cared for. And I exhaled my deepest internal energies, holistically touching the untouchable. Ah, the sweetness of that moment! The sweetness of that moment . . . The sweetness of that moment . . .

Sayings of the Sages

The taste [of truth is] beyond sweetness.
　　—*Dhammapada, 24*

Blessed are those who have not seen and yet have believed.
　　—*John 20:29*

A Hunk of Healing Humor

Some things have to be believed to be seen.
　　—*Ralph Hodgson on ESP*

Daily Affirmation

Once again, I taste the sweetness of coming to believe.

Twelve Step Thought

An angelic voice predicted my return, too: *resurrexit sicut dixit* or, "he was raised up as he said." And, in fact, an Almighty Power brought me out alive from the tomb of my addiction. For so long, I lay rigidly prone beneath the killing weight of an all-consuming obsession which petrified my soul. By the grace of a Power greater than myself, I was restored. In a way, I guess I was really reborn. Or maybe I just never truly lived before. It felt like I was washed clean with a very special kind of "sanity." Thus, I came to believe.

Sayings of the Sages

Turn us back to You, O Lord, and we will be restored.
     —*Lamentations 5:21*

He is risen from the dead.
     —*Matthew 28:7*

A Hunk of Healing Humor

The first requirement for immortality is death.
     —*Anonymous*

Daily Affirmation

I'm living this day as if it were my last.

Twelve Step Thought

In the darkest days of my disease, an addictive personality totally dominated my real self. Gruesomely, my life resembled a Jekyll and Hyde horror movie—*my* secret potion being a mixture of dependency and drugs. When I wasn't afflicted with a total blackout, the memories of my monstrous "Hyde" state filled me with shame. Yet I ran from shame and back to the magic elixir that wiped out painful memories. No power could save me. I dreamt many suicide scenarios. Then, at the moment of utmost despair, a ray of hope flashed an insight to my "Jekyll": "Seek help from a Twelve Step fellowship." Somehow, a Power greater than myself had begun restoring me to sanity.

Sayings of the Sages

The Devil cometh and soweth his seed in the man's heart.
    —*Theologia Germanica, XXV*

The sage seeks insight from chaos and doubt.
    —*Chuang Tsu: Inner Chapters, 2*

A Hunk of Healing Humor

Good taste is the excuse I've always given for leading such a bad life.
    —*Oscar Wilde*

Daily Affirmation

Deep down, I'm good and sane.

Twelve Step Thought

It took me so long to finally see that no person's power was greater than mine. Each person's ego constitutes a minute flash of light enmeshed in a universal field of pulsating, radiant splendor. After many years, I began to suspect that any human strengths were but part of a pattern of interconnected energy. Sensing a Power inconceivably greater than myself, I felt my center to be a junction point in a giant godly grid. Now, it seems there's a "me" on many levels and a "we" that's only one.

Sayings of the Sages

Anyone who has faith in me will do what I have been doing. He will do even greater things than these.
    —*John 14:12*

Approach the universe with Tao, and evil will have no power.
    —*Tao Te Ching, 60*

A Hunk of Healing Humor

McCabe's law: Nobody has to do anything.
    —*Charles McCabe*

Daily Affirmation

I am energized by a pattern of loving Power.

Twelve Step Thought

In some perverted way, I felt I knew better than others. The god of my youth had lost any relevance. My mind was *it*. (Only later did I realize I was stuck at the emotional level of midadolescence.) I shunned the spirit of my society that worshipped money and power. Both were beneath *my* dignity. My intellect would excel in the charitable arena of social services, bestowing relief on suffering sisters and brothers. In my thoughts I judged and condemned the heartless business types and politicians. To enlightened service, my brain said yes; my addiction said no. And damnably slowly, my self-righteous do-goodness crumbled into dust.

Sayings of the Sages

Do not judge, and you will not be judged.
> —*Luke 6:37*

We have not received the spirit of the world but the Spirit from God.
> —*I Corinthians 2:12*

A Hunk of Healing Humor

There is no such thing as justice—in or out of court.
> —*Clarence Darrow*

Daily Affirmation

My intellect has a Higher Power.

Twelve Step Thought

Yes, I wanted to better my condition. Toward the end of my addiction, my state was one of abject misery. Very often I just couldn't distinguish between sanity and insanity. In my warped mode, I believed achieving mental oblivion (i.e., "passing out") was the way to eliminate any emotional pain. Now it seems funny that I was brought low by becoming "high." Then, I quite seriously realized that my condition could be bettered; but, *only with help* from "outside" of myself.

Sayings of the Sages

Do not think of yourself as wise.
    —*Proverbs 3:7*

For the protection of the good, for the destruction of the wicked and for the establishment of righteousness, I come into being from age to age.
    —*Bhagavad Gita IV, 8*

A Hunk of Healing Humor

I have never let my schooling interfere with my education.
    —*Mark Twain*

Daily Affirmation

I find help easily beyond my little ego's boundaries.

Twelve Step Thought

At some point in recovery, *death* became more than a word. It became a mountainous obstacle to moving ahead with my life. More than any possible annihilation, I greatly feared running out of time before I could attain continual conscious contact with my Higher Power. I desperately wanted to reach the top of the mountain before darkness fell. Negative word-tapes kept playing in my head. Sidetracked by this fearful obsession, I was going out of my mind. Then, perhaps for the very first time, I really *heard* the Twelve Step words that only "a Power greater than ourselves could restore us to sanity."

Sayings of the Sages

The word was God. In him was life.
    —*John 1:1 & 4*

The words I have spoken to you are spirit and they are life.
    —*John 6:66*

A Hunk of Healing Humor

You don't die in the United States; you underachieve.
    —*Jerzy Kosinski*

Daily Affirmation

My Higher Power is moving me ahead.

Twelve Step Thought

Burning the candle at both ends once made sense to me. Before recovery, I closely clutched a passionate god of "do." What I really did was wallow in emotionalism and mistake it for real spiritual experience. Avoiding the actual divine "be," I made no distinction between feeling holy and being holy. I lived only to fan narcissistically the flames of my own foolish passion. In the end, my sickness snuffed out the glow of any inner sparks. A new fire had to be lit from the Eternal Flame. As I opened to this burning, I felt a holy fire that was cool and calm and . . . just was.

Sayings of the Sages

I AM has sent me to you.
  —*Exodus 3:14*

Light my lamp from your lamp.
  —*From a Sanskrit prayer*

A Hunk of Healing Humor

There is a crack in everything God has made.
  —*Ralph Waldo Emerson*

Daily Affirmation

Today, I'm burning with the gift of love.

Twelve Step Thought

For me, coming to believe was a vast voyage of discovery. Faith didn't just dawn suddenly. Rather, I had to walk a long, long way to get there. It was just like the Twelve Step prophets say it is: "You have to do the footwork." In a sense, I had to live as if faith were supporting me. I had to plod bravely ahead as if I knew where I was going. I got to live some other Program words: "Fake it until you make it." How paradoxical! Thanks to H.P., I began making it. And, in making it, I came to believe a Higher Power was helping me.

Sayings of the Sages

I will walk on the main road and my only fear will be of straying from it.
—*Tao Te Ching, 53*

Man could not without God, and God should not without man.
—*Theologia Germanica, III*

A Hunk of Healing Humor

I would rather be a coward than brave, because people hurt you when you are brave.
—*E. M. Forster*

Daily Affirmation

I'm doing the indicated footwork, and making it.

Twelve Step Thought

My addictiveness is still a stumbling block that I frequently trip over. Rather, I should say that I often stub my psychic "toe" on one of the many protrusions of my obsessive personality. Sometimes, it even seems that I obsess as many times as other people breathe. Always when this happens, I am fixated quite selfishly on my poor little personhood. When this kind of fixation hurts me enough, then I recall there is a Power greater than myself. I'm able to look beyond myself for the assistance to become restored. I renew my faith in H.P.

Sayings of the Sages

To be obsessed by the idea of freedom . . . is itself a form of slavery.
　　　—*Idries Shah, Reflections*

The end of desire is the end of sorrow.
　　　—*Dhammapada, 24*

A Hunk of Healing Humor

When we remember that we are all mad, the mysteries disappear and life stands explained.
　　　—*Mark Twain*

Daily Affirmation

Today, I'm totally focused on my Higher Power.

Twelve Step Thought

At the beginning of my recovery, I was reminded in a refreshingly different way that there is a God and that this God loves me unconditionally. Also, this God desires my highest happiness. More than "restoring" me from my burned-out state, this Power would bless me with divine bliss. Since I admired the serenity of my advisers, I really came to believe there is a Supreme Being who wants only the best for me. So I determined that, since I seem to be gifted with an addictive personality, I'll just seek the ultimate "high" of cosmic consciousness.

Sayings of the Sages

Goodness and kindness pursue me every day of my life.
—*Psalm 23:6*

Accordingly, if you who are wicked know how to give good gifts to your children, how much more will your heavenly father give the holy spirit to those who ask him!
—*Luke 11:13*

A Hunk of Healing Humor

Father expected a good deal from God. He didn't actually accuse God of inefficiency, but when he prayed his tone was loud and angry, like that of a dissatisfied guest in a carelessly managed hotel.
—*Clarence Shepard Day*

Daily Affirmation

God wants only the best for me.

Twelve Step Thought

Amid all my growing pains, I have been graced with a few revelations in recovery. For example, if this power-greater-than-myself indeed is a spiritual being, he/she/it would hardly be interested in the smoothness of my skin or in the luxuriousness of my automobile or in my job status or in the size of my bank account. How often I forget this reality! More likely, an unlimited Divine Spirit would be tuned in to the state of my soul—seeing whether or not I'm peaceful, trusting, accepting, loving. There is a message in this truth for me.

Sayings of the Sages

Teach me good sense and knowledge.
    —*Psalm 119:66*

Carrying body and soul and embracing the one, can you avoid separation?
    —*Tae Te Ching, 10*

A Hunk of Healing Humor

God is dead, but fifty thousand social workers have risen to take his place.
    —*J. D. McCoughey*

Daily Affirmation

Today, I'm peaceful, accepting, and loving.

Twelve Step Thought

Now I understand that the level of faith expressed in the Second Step will have to be affirmed again and again and again. I've discovered that my life patterns are not so easily changed. I don't grow instantly or once-and-for-all. The progress I've experienced is actually in the *rate* of growth. It seems it's a one-day-at-a-time process that ends only when I die. Yet, more and more, I feel the pace of growth accelerate. Because I forget, I need to proclaim periodically that there is a Power greater than myself. In fact, I must renew (at ever-higher levels) the holistic adventure of coming to believe.

Sayings of the Sages

Where were you when I laid the earth's foundations?
    —*Job 38:4*

A man of disciplined mind . . . attains purity of spirit.
    —*Bhagavad Gita II, 64*

A Hunk of Healing Humor

I am an atheist, thank God!
    —*Anonymous*

Daily Affirmation

I'm growing more today than yesterday.

Twelve Step Thought

Leap Year is a good epoch-marker for a thrust forward in the quality of being. It's time to really believe and actively trust that a Higher Power is paving the way to making me truly whole. Previously, my depending just on myself and my inadequacies acted as an anchor which kept me looping in vicious circles. Somehow, I preferred the known dizziness of addiction to the unknown movement that followed letting go. Then, in a moment of supreme crisis, I let grace snap my anchor chain. Ever since, a divine current has swept me relentlessly toward the shore of total liberation. Springing from divine energy, I leap now for cosmic consciousness.

Sayings of the Sages

When it is made known, we shall be like him.
—*I John 3:2*

Seek the highest consciousness.
—*Dhammapada, 14*

A Hunk of Healing Humor

If a man should happen to reach perfection in this world, he would have to die immediately to enjoy himself.
—*Josh Billings*

Daily Affirmation

A divine current is carrying me along.

Twelve Step Thought

After being buffeted long enough by the raging winds of my obsession, I decided to turn my riotous will and my shattered life over to the care of a spiritual guide. At the time, I don't think I understood (nor do I *really* understand now) just what spirit-being was involved. Anything had to be better than my personal hell. Throwing myself on the mercy of a (hopefully) saving strength, I was plucked from the shameful abyss. Now I ask and trust that that Power cares for me.

Sayings of the Sages

If anyone thirsts, let him come to me and drink.
        —*John 7:37*

I am thy pupil; teach me who am seeking refuge in Thee.
        —*Bhagavad Gita II, 7*

A Hunk of Healing Humor

A man without religion is like a fish without a bicycle.
        —*Arthur Bloch*

Daily Affirmation

Today's events are in the care of my Higher Power.

Twelve Step Thought

My way only reinforced deep-down feelings of inadequacy. My way provided painful sessions with a psychiatrist. My way saw the splitting apart of a family and the loss of much-loved children. My way frittered away a few worthwhile friendships. My telling God how things had to be led me to fight the flow of life's events —often pounding my head against a stone wall. Even so, I foolishly resisted turning my will and my life over to the care of a Higher Power. Now, on a bit-by-bit basis, I become willing to go beyond myself.

Sayings of the Sages

If, from time to time, you give up expectations, you will be able to perceive what it is you are getting.
    —*Idries Shah, Reflections*

Yielding is the way of the Tao.
    —*Tao Te Ching, 40*

A Hunk of Healing Humor

Too many people miss the silver lining because they're expecting gold.
    —*Maurice Seitter*

Daily Affirmation

My Higher Power leads the way.

Twelve Step Thought

For me, "to turn over" meant giving up ownership. I saw the act as handing it all over—disclaiming pleasure as well as pain, joy as well as unhappiness. The opposite state no longer held any attraction. On the contrary, the possessiveness of my obsession had just about done me in. My belief in the possibility of possessing anything turned out to be a tremendous illusion. And I now have a burning desire to avoid all that is illusory. Gradually, I've come to discover that I'm merely a conscious passer-through of some Greater Power—in whose care I place my will and my life.

Sayings of the Sages

Into your hands I commit my spirit.
  —*Psalm 31:5*

Understand that the body is merely the foam of a wave, the shadow of a shadow. Snap the flower arrows of desire and then, unseen, escape the king of death.
  —*Dhammapada, 4*

A Hunk of Healing Humor

Satan hasn't a single salaried helper; the Opposition employ a million.
  —*Mark Twain*

Daily Affirmation

I'm placing my life in God's care today.

Twelve Step Thought

"Made a decision" is a shorter and sweeter wording of my more complex statement: I opted for relief after enduring much infliction, consternation, confusion, seeming-resolution, mortification, and tribulation. I didn't just decide. I dragged myself to this decision on my hands and knees, begging some force beyond my ego to save me. I admitted that I was beaten. I somehow trusted that a Power greater than myself could relieve my insanity. And I decided to ask for help. In that mindset I ran to a Twelve Step Program. This action, born of my decision, reinforced turning over control of my life.

Sayings of the Sages

A path is formed by walking on it.
—*Chuang Tsu: Inner Chapters, 2*

Seek the Lord while he is still to be found, call to him while he is still near. Let the wicked man . . . turn back to the Lord who will take pity on him, to our God who is rich in forgiving.
—*Isaiah 55:6 & 7*

A Hunk of Healing Humor

I like life. It's something to do.
—*Ronnie Shakes*

Daily Affirmation

I ask God for help with all my duties today.

Twelve Step Thought

Early on I feared that really turning it over to a Greater Power would erase my newfound and gradually building positive self-image. Following years of imprisonment in a cage of negativity and self-doubt, I was anxious not to lose this fledgling constructive perception. Surprisingly, I came to discover that, by renouncing independence at my innermost core, I transcend my self-boundaries and am truly free. I learned that the Power constantly sustains my conscious center just as the sun is always shining. When I turn away, like the earth from its star, I face only my own shadow.

Sayings of the Sages

For all who are enlightened by the True Light can never more be deceived.
　　　—*Theologia Germanica, XL*

Live in the way and the light will grow in you.
　　　—*Dhammapada, 2*

A Hunk of Healing Humor

Don't be agnostic—be something.
　　　—*Robert Frost*

Daily Affirmation

Today I will bask in the sunshine of my Higher Power.

Twelve Step Thought

"As I understand God" is not necessarily saying much. Yet, restating the words to "as God understands me" says much more than I can possibly encompass. This is no flip exercise. In the seeking of a transcendent reality, "understanding" goes far beyond intellectual analysis. Rather, it's the *experiential* knowing of God that I now seek. Or maybe it seeks me. Always, as the fingers of my spirit start to close around the divine being, the comprehension of divinity slips away from me. Fortunately, the concept of a Higher Power allows me to touch God in my Twelve Step support group.

Sayings of the Sages

The blind cannot appreciate beautiful patterns, the deaf cannot hear the sounds of bells and drums.
    —*Chuang Tsu: Inner Chapters, 1*

Lord God, the almighty, who was and is and is to come.
    —*Revelation 4:8*

A Hunk of Healing Humor

Is man one of God's blunders or is God one of man's?
    —*Friedrich Nietzsche*

Daily Affirmation

I touch God in my Twelve Step group.

Twelve Step Thought

Flitting through shadowy fields of duality,
I cling so hard to my old personality.
The breath of spiritlife blows;
Yet, I don't lean to the wind.
Let go . . . into Spirit's flow!
Fear of dying grips my mind.
What if my "me" melts into a little pool at God's feet?
That's good for God's amusement, but not for my
psyche, yet.
And yet . . . and yet . . . letting go's my only serenity.

Sayings of the Sages

Those who conquer do so because they yield.
        —*Tao Te Ching, 61*

Give up the old ways.
        —*Dhammapada, 1*

A Hunk of Healing Humor

I'm not afraid to die. I just don't want to be there when
it happens.
        —*Woody Allen*

Daily Affirmation

Letting go is my serenity.

Twelve Step Thought

Playing "guts ball" is what I call turning something over to the care of a Higher Power. This is *serious* business for me. It takes all my willingness for most of my ego-wants and my life to be given up to some Supreme Being's providence. At first, it was a big gamble on a remotely possible payoff. But, I had not much else to lose and who knows how much to gain. I was like one of Don Juan's disciples, as related by Carlos Castenada: I had to jump off a cliff, expecting that a divine power would keep me from falling. And, without my knowing how, it worked. Quite obviously, here I am: whole, happier, more peaceful, and certainly cared for.

Sayings of the Sages

I put my flesh between my teeth, I take my life in my hands.
    —*Job 13:14*

Thus speaks the Most High, whose home is in eternity, whose name is holy: "I live in a high and holy place, but I am also with the contrite and humbled spirit, to give the humbled spirit new life, to revive contrite hearts."
    —*Isaiah 57:15*

A Hunk of Healing Humor

It's so nice to see people with plenty of get-up-and-go, especially if some of them are visiting you.
    —*Herbert Prochnow*

Daily Affirmation

I'm betting on my Higher Power today.

Twelve Step Thought

Often, at Twelve Step meetings, I've heard that satisfying and enduring recovery is maintained *only* through ever-renewed surrender to a Higher Power. For me, this involves admitting to the total inadequacy of my ego by itself. Practically, it means giving up control over people, places, and things. To find any serenity, I find it necessary to turn over the outcomes of all events in my life to God. In my own way, I'm trying to prefer the Divine Will to my little will. Of course, I frequently don't succeed in this purpose. Yet, I offer my efforts as a sacrifice to that Power which blesses me constantly.

Sayings of the Sages

Do thy work as a sacrifice, becoming free from all attachment.
          —*Bhagavad Gita III, 9*

Take thy stand upon an utter abandonment of thyself.
          —*Theologia Germanica, VIII*

A Hunk of Healing Humor

God is not a cosmic bell-boy for whom we can press a button to get things.
          —*Harry Emerson Fosdick*

Daily Affirmation

All outcomes belong to my Higher Power.

Twelve Step Thought

Over the years and on a very gradual basis, I've turned over ever more of life and will to my Higher Power. It's really been a one-day-at-a-time progression. Even so, I often wanted perfection *now*! Father Time and Mother Nature have disabused me of this notion. I found that only eternity comes all at once. For me, trust in the divine will takes practice; and practice requires discipline. Then, disciplined practice leads to the habit of being in God's care. I find myself stringing a lot of little acts together like making a garland of many flowers.

Sayings of the Sages

Like garlands woven from a heap of flowers, fashion from your life as many good deeds.
　　—Dhammapada, 4

Look after me, God, I take shelter in you.
　　—Psalm 16:1

A Hunk of Healing Humor

The harder you work, the luckier you get.
　　—Gary Player

Daily Affirmation

I'm turning one situation at a time over to my Higher Power.

Twelve Step Thought

A FABLE ON FOOLISHNESS

As children bring their broken toys
 With tears for us to mend,
 I brought my broken dreams to God,
 Because He was my friend.
 But then, instead of leaving Him in peace to work
alone,
 I hung around and tried to help, with ways that were
my own.
 At last I snatched them back and cried,
 "How can You be so slow?"
 "My child," He said,
 "What could I do? You never did let go."

Sayings of the Sages

We all know people who want water to be wetter.
 —*Idries Shah, Reflections*

Who can wait quietly while the mud settles? Who can
remain still until the moment of action? Observers of
the Tao do not seek fulfillment. Not seeking fulfillment,
they are not swayed by desire for change.
 —*Tao Te Ching, 15*

A Hunk of Healing Humor

God is a comedian whose audience is afraid to laugh.
 —*H. L. Mencken*

Daily Affirmation

Today, I'm leaving my hopes in God's hands.

Twelve Step Thought

For many years, during and following my addiction, I felt that my life was an overpowering burden which I carefully avoided carrying. I found some escape in many cycles of obsession and compulsion. In fact, I was one "sick cookie." Even so, as I honestly reached for the Force within me, I found that this Source of strength began to manage and rule over all my doings without perpetuating any of my previous mistakes. Consequently, I simply learned to accept what I was given by my Higher Power. Looking back now, I clearly see that God supported me much beyond my wildest expectations.

Sayings of the Sages

Unload your burden on God, and he will support you.
   —*Psalm 55:22*

He accepted what he was given with delight, and when it was gone, he gave it no more thought. This is called not using the mind against Tao and not using man to help heaven. Such was the true man.
   —*Chuang Tsu: Inner Chapters, 6*

A Hunk of Healing Humor

Millions long for immortality who don't know what to do on a rainy Sunday afternoon.
   —*Susan Ertz*

Daily Affirmation

My Higher Power supports me beyond my wildest expectations.

Twelve Step Thought

A wise recovering addict once said that the Third Step is a pathway to a belief system that really works. For me, this means deciding to turn my will and my life over to the care of my Higher Power. Getting to the path is the basic thrust of Step One and Step Two. And starting to walk on the way is what Step Three is about for me. Using Step Three on an ongoing basis is like using a flashlight to find my way through a dark alley. The practice helps me not to stumble over so many obstacles. Yet, I do get sidetracked fairly often. That's when a spiritual sponsor helps me to get back on course.

Sayings of the Sages

Keeping to the main road is easy, but people love to get sidetracked.
  —*Tao Te Ching, 53*

Surrendering in thought all actions to me.
  —*Bhagavad Gita XVII, 57*

Hunk of Healing Humor

Nothing gives you quite the thrill as treading in the darkness on a step that isn't there.
  —*Herbert Prochnow*

Daily Affirmation

I'm getting feedback from my sponsor to stay on course.

Twelve Step Thought

When I began recovery, working Step Three appropriately required a lot of guidance from someone who was well along in the process. After all, how much experience did *I* have really in turning my life and my will over to the care of a Supreme Being? Shucks, oftentimes I couldn't get out of my own way! So the errors I made with the Third Step caused me a lot of pain. Fortunately, I was spared many more mistakes, because I listened ever increasingly to the advice of a Twelve Step guide who had already learned important lessons about practicing this step. I give thanks to God for recovering peers who prodded me along.

Sayings of the Sages

Now, if we ought to be, and desire to be obedient and submit unto God, we must also submit to what we receive at the hands of any of his creatures, or our submission is all false.
—*Theologia Germanica, XXXV*

If the traveler can find a virtuous and wise companion, let him go with him joyfully and overcome the dangers of the way.
—*Dhammapada, 23*

A Hunk of Healing Humor

A kleptomaniac is a person who helps himself because he can't help himself.
—*Henry Morgan*

Daily Affirmation

Today, I'm taking the advice of a Twelve Step guide.

Twelve Step Thought

After much program involvement, I discovered that "turning over" means *turning toward* God. Somehow, I found a godly connection within the innermost regions of my heart. Until I truly turn to my Higher Power, I'm at least somewhat upset by the happenings of my day. And "turning to" simply is calling for help from the Source of all strength. In fact, for Step Three, "deciding" is in itself a form of prayer. Once I've prayed, it somehow becomes a little easier to face a tremendous nothingness that sometimes fills my days.

Sayings of the Sages

Wherever you are, wherever you go, you are miserable unless you turn to God.
— *Thomas a Kempis*

All who call on the name of God will be saved.
— *Joel 2:22*

A Hunk of Healing Humor

An atheist is a man who has no invisible means of support.
— *Fulton Sheen*

Daily Affirmation

God makes my nothing something.

Twelve Step Thought

For a long while, I cried out in anguish for help —with no apparent response from above! Instead, I seemed to be further burdened by depression and even despair. I felt abandoned by that very Power I had tried so desperately to reach. Slowly, I came to realize that no Supreme Spirit could be found on the level where I had been seeking. In truth, the Divine Mother has always held my soul's hand. Only *I* was insensitive to that transcendent touch. So, though my body will fade like all clothing, the (now hidden) brilliance of my spirit will never be diminished. Now I finally see that, to have reached this realization, the Loving Source showered me with blessings all along.

Sayings of the Sages

Know thou for certain that My devotee never perishes.
    —*Bhagavad Gita IX, 31*

From the fullness of his grace, we have all received one blessing after another.
    —*John 1:16*

A Hunk of Healing Humor

In these times you have to be an optimist to open your eyes in the morning.
    —*Carl Sandburg*

Daily Affirmation

I'm constantly being showered with blessings.

Twelve Step Thought

The days of my active addiction were filled with tension, discomfort and restlessness. This dis-ease of mine meant a state of un-ease. This condition characterized all the discombobulated events of my sad existence. So I saw that, along with praying or trying to turn over my will and life, I needed to insert some "ease" into my reality. Gradually, I learned some new values: relaxing and letting go of outcomes. I finally got in touch with the fact that I'm being cared for totally, guided along just as the Apostle of Ireland was brought from slave with nothing to Archbishop with a see at Armagh.

Sayings of the Sages

Let your mind wander in the pure and simple. Be one with the infinite. Allow all things to take their course. Do not try to be clever.

  —*Chuang Tsu: Inner Chapters, 7*

Hope is not "Have I got a chance?" It is more often: "Have I seen my chance?"

  —*Idries Shah, Reflections*

A Hunk of Healing Humor

We are restless because of incessant change, but we would be frightened if change were stopped.

  —*Lyman Lloyd Bryson*

Daily Affirmation

Today, I'm enjoying the divine gift of ease.

Twelve Step Thought

Mahatma Gandhi once said that there is more to life than increasing its speed. In my own case, getting to turn my will and life over means slowing down. When my mind is racing at escape velocity, I'm unable to release control for any reason. And willingness isn't sufficient. I really must slow my pace—even as the world in which I live spins faster and faster. Somehow, I need to stop and to get my bearings. When my mind becomes still, how-it-all-works becomes so clear to me. Then, it's relatively easy for me to decide to place all of my being in the care of Divine Good, of the Eternal Lifeforce.

Sayings of the Sages

If we are to ascribe all goodness to the One Eternal Good, as of right and truth we ought, so must we also of right and truth ascribe unto Him the beginning, middle, and end of our course, so that nothing remains to man or the creature.
  —*Theologia Germanica, LIII*

Stillness and tranquillity set things in order in the universe.
  —*Tao Te Ching, 45*

A Hunk of Healing Humor

Any idiot can face a crisis—it's this day-to-day living that wears you out.
  —*Anton Chekhov*

Daily Affirmation

I'm slowing down and seeing clearly.

Twelve Step Thought

Step Three is an affirmation asking for *action*. In fact, I've been told quite often that acting rightly is the only way to reduce self-will (self-will is the exact opposite of the Third Step). In the business of debunking my ego, "into action" is the best advice given. Anyway, sitting in some corner just generates depression. What is essential is the willingness to keep moving, progressing. And, beyond the press of flesh, the siren of psyche calls to me so sweetly—capturing me with ever-less resistance. Swaying to heavenly music, I'm hypnotized by the unconscious undulations of my soul.

Sayings of the Sages

Do what has to be done and give no thought to yourself.
—*Chuang Tsu: Inner Chapters, 4*

Do your work with mastery.
—*Dhammapada, 26*

A Hunk of Healing Humor

I do not like work even when someone else does it.
—*Mark Twain*

Daily Affirmation

Today, I'm moving and progressing.

Twelve Step Thought

Well into recovery, I found that my ego (my little self) is totally self-serving. "Turn over control? You must be crazy!" In my egotistical view of the world, I see myself as "better" than everyone else. I certainly couldn't see leaving all outcomes up to God. *I* had to strive. Yet, along with my obsessiveness and my addiction, my ego caused me nothing but grief. After one serious life crisis, I made the decision to turn my will and my life over to the care of a loving divinity. In so doing, I found a giant Self in which I could immerse myself.

Sayings of the Sages

Not my will, but yours be done.
    —*Luke 22:42*

The more a man followeth after his own self-will, and self-will groweth in him, the farther off he is from the true Good.
    —*Theologia Germanica, XXXIV*

A Hunk of Healing Humor

The only cure for vanity is laughter; and the only fault that's laughable is vanity.
    —*Henri Bergson*

Daily Affirmation

My giant Self is a constant source of strength.

Twelve Step Thought

Turning over my will implies being willing to forgive whoever attacks or seems to be attacking me. Responding with an angry retort or holding on to hurt indicates that I don't really trust that a Higher Power is caring for me. Yet, God doesn't care in dribs and drabs. Eternal Energy always is taking care of me—without *any* interruption. And, to truly experience this reality, I find that I actually have to *let go* somewhere in the process of talking about turning things over. Because the outcome of any situation really is in God's hands, I can forgive anyone. Who am I to question how the Divine Director finishes the scene? I'm finding that the only effective answer to anger is love.

Sayings of the Sages

If you do not forgive men their wrongdoings, your Father will not forgive your wrongdoings.
—*Matthew 6:15*

Peter came to Jesus and asked, "Lord, how many times shall I forgive my brother when he sins against me? Up to seven times?" Jesus answered, "I tell you, not seven times, but seventy times seven."
—*Matthew 18:21 & 22*

A Hunk of Healing Humor

Always forgive your enemies—nothing annoys them so much.
—*Oscar Wilde*

Daily Affirmation

Today, I'm responding to anger with love.

Twelve Step Thought

Now, I understand God to be total good and love unlimited. Yet, I didn't always see things this way. For a long while, God was completely beyond my reach. And I *was* reaching—perhaps too painstakingly! Then, I saw God as the avenger and the punisher who was paying me back for all my weaknesses and mistakes. So, my reaction: "The hell with you." I determined to pull myself up by my own bootstraps. This led to utter failure. Finally, being absolutely desperate and dangling perilously before death's door, I found nowhere else to turn. So I cried: "Please help me, God." And, little by little, I experienced the sweet and soulsoothing lovingness of the divine response.

Sayings of the Sages

Have you noticed how many people who walk in the shade curse the sun?
—*Idries Shah, Reflections*

I would fain be to the Eternal Goodness, what his own hand is to a man.
—*Theologia Germanica, X*

A Hunk of Healing Humor

If triangles had a God, he would have three sides.
—*Montesquieu*

Daily Affirmation

Help me, God, in all I do.

Twelve Step Thought

Learning to forgive others (and myself) has been the tough part of turning my will over to a Higher Power. I remember being at a meeting one evening. In a joking manner, I asked a woman if she was behaving herself. Her husband interpreted my action as a "pass." He spit some angry and nasty comments in my face. Surprised and jolted, I simply said, "Sorry you feel that way," and walked away. With turmoil brewing in my gut, I decided to turn this situation over to H.P. Then, I focused on mentally beaming forgiveness and love at my accuser. Within ten minutes, love and joy suffused my whole being. (And the husband apologized at the next meeting.)

Sayings of the Sages

Little children, let us not love with word or tongue but with action and with truth. This then is how we know that we belong to the truth, and how we set our hearts at rest in his presence.
    —*I John 3:18 & 19*

Why should I mind whether or not people approve of my words? People call this childlike. This is what I call being a follower of heaven.
    —*Chuang Tsu: Inner Chapters, 4*

A Hunk of Healing Humor

When angry, count four; when very angry, swear.
    —*Mark Twain*

Daily Affirmation

Today, I'm beaming love at all who hurt me.

Twelve Step Thought

Totally trusting in the care of a loving God means preoccupying myself with a special state of grace. Immersion in my Higher Power's energy field completely cleanses me of all fear, guilt, and anger. Why? Maybe because trust is based on the experience of being helped before. Despite the terrors of my addiction and my numerous character defects, I was gifted with a state of recovery. I actually felt tremendous moral burdens being lifted from me. I sensed depression being transformed into joy. I perceived grandiosity being converted into reasoned assertiveness. Best of all, I knew the immersive baptism of two Twelve Step programs had saved my life. Who was I to doubt anymore?

Sayings of the Sages

Daniel was . . . found to be quite unhurt, because he had trusted in his God.
   —*Daniel 6:23*

The Tao alone nourishes and brings everything to fulfillment.
   —*Tao Te Ching, 41*

A Hunk of Healing Humor

God will forgive me. That's his business.
   —*Heinrich Heine*

Daily Affirmation

My Higher Power will get me through any difficulty.

Twelve Step Thought

Embracing recovery is the only way that I'll stay recovered. Addiction is so cunning, devious, and powerful! Fortunately, I'm not alone. There's a Higher Power I can turn to. The addictiveness only attacks me when I feel completely isolated. Sometimes, my ego still leads me to think that I'm facing impossible odds or (more horrible) the unbearable weight of tedium all alone. By some spiritual blessing, I now often remember that a love-filled Supreme Being unfailingly supports this fragile world. Then, I know that I must run to embrace my Higher Power. When I'm consciously wrapped in those divine arms, the odious darkness is transformed into loving light.

Sayings of the Sages

If there be true Love along with his knowledge, he cannot but cleave to God, and forsake all that is not God or of Him.
—*Theologia Germanica, XLI*

The true light is that Eternal Light which is God; or else it is a created light, but yet divine, which is called grace. And these are both the true Light.
—*Theologia Germanica, XXXI*

A Hunk of Healing Humor

Religion is a way of walking, not a way of talking.
—*William R. Inge*

Daily Affirmation

My Higher Power is always there to back me up.

Twelve Step Thought

Many moons into recovery, I finally discovered experientially that my decisions are made only in the *here* and *now*. Previously, I spent a lot of time thinking about making a decision in the future. Of course, this old practice in no way altered the extent of my misery. I just never could turn to a Higher Power in the future. And, although I released much of my past, I never could count on a Divine Providence existing in the past. Rather, I have to actually *be* in the present to effectively decide anything. In fact, it required much determination and persistent trying (as in "Fake it till you make it") to arrive at deciding this very second to place my fate in God's hands.

Sayings of the Sages

Better to live one moment in the moment of the way beyond the way.
—*Dhammapada, 8*

The wise who have united their intelligence [with the Divine] renouncing the fruits which their action yields and freed from the bonds of birth reach the sorrowless state.
—*Bhagavad Gita II, 51*

A Hunk of Healing Humor

Providence protects children and idiots. I know because I have tested it.
—*Mark Twain*

Daily Affirmation

I'm experiencing Divine Providence right now.

Twelve Step Thought

Not so long ago, I was worrying about replacing the dependence of addiction with the dependence on/of a Twelve Step program. Maybe I was just reflecting the concern expressed by some psychiatrists and psychologists: that one dependency problem was really being replaced by another dependency problem. Others told me that dependence on a Higher Power is the *means* to gain true independence of spirit. Many who mentioned this to me appeared to be quite happy. The joyous recovering ones definitely served as models for me. And, paradoxically, I found that this kind of "dependence" became my main source of strength.

Sayings of the Sages

Consider how well he has treated you; loudly give him thanks.
　　　—Tobit 13:6

I wish to go forward and get nearer to the Eternal Goodness.
　　　—Theologia Germanica, X

A Hunk of Healing Humor

Liberty doesn't work as well in practice as it does in speeches.
　　　—Will Rogers

Daily Affirmation

Depending on my Higher Power gives me great independence.

Twelve Step Thought

Quite often I've made the decision to "turn it over." I make this decision so frequently because I keep "taking it back." Consistency of giving up control was never one of my strong points. At times, I seemed to follow a yo-yo course of turning over and taking back. Yet, by persistently making this crucial decision, my negative attitude has been evolving into wholesome and constructive thinking. Also, very gradually, I came to realize that *I* am the *one* who can make this decision to exert myself. There has to be an impetus for action and some exertion on my part. Then, my Higher Power graciously supports my decisiveness.

Sayings of the Sages

If we are content with whatever happens and follow the flow, joy and sorrow cannot affect us. This is what the ancients called freedom from bondage.
—*Chuang Tsu: Inner Chapters, 6*

Make your ways known to me, teach me your paths. Set me in the way of your truth, and teach me, for you are the God who saves me.
—*Psalm 25:4 & 5*

A Hunk of Healing Humor

Progress might have been all right once, but it's gone on too long.
—*Ogden Nash*

Daily Affirmation

Today, I'm giving up control to my Higher Power.

Twelve Step Thought

My making a decision meant stepping onto the path with a heart and beginning to live a life based on responding to love's promptings. It even meant that I postulated love as the response to all questions and all challenges. Ultimately, this way uses love as a springboard to attain the Source of all love. It especially includes listening ever so carefully for the softly spoken directions emanating from the loving energy field of the Eternal Lover. In the West, the divine whisper is called *grace*; in the East, *shakti*. From whatever direction they emanate, these holy utterances are what guide me home to the nameless spawning point of Life's longing for itself.

Sayings of the Sages

The way is not in the sky. The way is in the heart. See how you love whatever keeps you from your journey. All things arise and pass away. But the awakened awake forever.
    —*Dhammapada, 18*

We know that we have passed from death to life, because we love our brothers. Anyone who does not love remains in death.
    —*I John 3:14*

A Hunk of Healing Humor

He that falls in love with himself will have no rivals.
    —*Benjamin Franklin*

Daily Affirmation

I'm listening carefully for the loving divine whisper.

Twelve Step Thought

Even while recovering from my obsessions, I found that life was still unmanageable. Problems other than those related to addictions needed to be turned over too. In short, my prior philosophical position of self-sufficiency proved to be quite improbable. For me, contented recovery is found only through God's help *after* much self-sacrifice and learning of painful lessons. Somehow, I must pass successfully between the Scylla and Charybdis of impulsiveness and procrastination. In so doing, I believe I'll find how letting go is the way. And, in so doing, my understanding of a Higher Power will grow tremendously.

Sayings of the Sages

In whatsoever creature the Perfect shall be known, therein creature-nature, qualities, the I, the self and the like, must all be lost.
        —*Theologia Germanica, I*

Through selfless action, [the sage] attains fulfillment.
        —*Tao Te Ching, 7*

A Hunk of Healing Humor

We are all born mad. Some remain so.
        —*Samuel Beckett*

Daily Affirmation

Today, I'll have it my Higher Power's way.

Twelve Step Thought

How often I've wished I had more will power! Now I see that the answer to truly living my life has little to do with having "more." The real answer is right-willing. In fact, I use my will rightly when it conforms to God's will. The most workable approach that I know is best summarized by the Serenity Prayer: "God grant me the serenity to accept the things I cannot change, courage to change the things I can, and wisdom to know the difference." This moving petition expresses the eternal spiritual values. And, after I was awakened spiritually, my Twelve Step programs began to help me realize my goal of spiritual growth.

Sayings of the Sages

Let him gain, little by little, tranquillity.
  —*Bhagavad Gita VI, 25*

Put on the new self, created to be like God.
  —*Ephesians 4:24*

A Hunk of Healing Humor

I am better than my reputation.
  —*Friedrich von Schiller*

Daily Affirmation

My Higher Power is granting me serenity.

Twelve Step Thought

As soon as I could, I conducted a thorough and honest inventory of my situation. My overall assessment: *all* the emotional earthquakes in my life were due to a major fault called an unhealthy ego. In my case, its shifting and prancing produced a lot of paranoia. Throughout the difficult, visceral process of writing down character faults and personal quagmires, I buoyed myself with the belief that self-knowledge is a basic ingredient of emotional and spiritual development. Fearing to look closely, I asked my Higher Power for the necessary strength.

Sayings of the Sages

Verily the renunciation of any duty that ought to be done is not right.
—*Bhagavad Gita XVIII, 7*

Accept misfortune as the *human* condition.
—*Tao Te Ching, 13*

A Hunk of Healing Humor

May bad fortune follow you all your days. And never catch up with you!
—*Quoted by Herbert Prochnow*

Daily Affirmation

I rely on the strength of my Higher Power.

Twelve Step Thought

For an inventory to be truly *searching* and *fearless*, it *must* be written. I discovered this truth (much to my dismay) quite some time after joining a Twelve Step organization. Previously, I thought that talking courageously about my character traits in front of my fellow addicts was more than sufficient. Rationalization reigns again! Because I hadn't done any serious writing, many points were missed or glossed over. So I faced the music later on when I *had* to write out a Fourth Step for peace of mind. And, remembering the trauma attached, it was a lot harder for me to do a *fearless* inventory later on in recovery.

Sayings of the Sages

Write, therefore, the things which you have seen, and the things which are.
    —*Revelation 1:19*

Words are not eternal. Because of words, there are distinctions.
    —*Chuang Tsu: Inner Chapters, 2*

A Hunk of Healing Humor

When ideas fail, words come in very handy.
    —*Goethe*

Daily Affirmation

Today, I fearlessly update my inventory.

Twelve Step Thought

When I look deep inside, I see fear as a sort of spirit-shark, ripping apart the flesh of my serenity. In believing that others can attack me, I alone give birth to this metaphorical beast deep in the bowels of my being. Upon close examination, I even find myself attacking others to prevent an anticipated attack of my person. From such depths of insanity, only a Higher Power could rescue me.

Sayings of the Sages

There is no fear in love. But perfect love drives out fear, because fear has to do with punishment.
    —*I John 4:18*

Your real problem is that you are a member of the human race. Face that one first.
    —*Idries Shah, Reflections*

A Hunk of Healing Humor

Nobody ever died of laughter.
    —*Max Beerbohm*

Daily Affirmation

Today, my Higher Power evaporates my fears.

Twelve Step Thought

Finally putting a Fourth Step into writing served as a symbol of my complete willingness to move forward. My growth required the supreme effort of committing all my personality flaws *and* my positive aspects to words on a page. In so doing, I greatly reinforced my determination to change and began listening intently to love's promptings. And I found that loving is letting go of fear. Prior to this course of action, I was more or less stagnating in my recovery program. Now, I can see how rapidly I'm growing. And, as my thoughts flow onto paper, I see ever more clearly what still impedes my progress.

Sayings of the Sages

If we confess our sins, he is faithful and just and will forgive us our sins and purify us from all unrighteousness.

—*I John 1:9*

Bless the Lord, my soul, and remember all his kindnesses: in forgiving all your offenses, in curing all your diseases.

—*Psalm 103:2 & 3*

A Hunk of Healing Humor

It is base to snatch a purse, daring to embezzle a million, but it is great beyond measure to steal a crown. The sin lessens as the guilt increases.

—*Johann von Schiller*

Daily Affirmation

I'm checking my progress by putting it in writing.

Twelve Step Thought

Early on in the process of mending, a friend recommended that I keep a diary or journal describing my progress on the spiritually valued journey to a state of health and wholeness. From this exercise, I eventually learned that writing about the status of my soul is a form of prayer. In noting steps forward and backward, I get better in touch with the deepest part of me. In the last analysis, I'm forced to find an effective Higher Power within myself. By putting it in writing, I more easily see the necessary steps along the way. So, by honestly journaling, I succeed in tracking a wonderful way of living.

Sayings of the Sages

The prayer offered in faith will make the sick person well.

—James 5:15

Nothing grieveth him but his own guilt and wickedness; for that is not right and is contrary to God, and for that cause he is grieved and troubled in spirit. This is what is meant by true repentance for sin.

—Theologia Germanica, XI

A Hunk of Healing Humor

Get your facts first, and then you can distort them as you please.

—Mark Twain

Daily Affirmation

In journaling, I'm tracking a wonderful way of living.

Twelve Step Thought

After some years in recovery, I started to understand that Step Four is just the beginning of a very personal and positive lifetime practice. I found it takes time to get rid of character faults and to master avoiding the development of new ones. My initial Fourth Step was really the first step on a long road to gaining ultimate meaning in my life. It's a lengthy process of sidestepping that which is bad for me and of seeking that which is good for me. Without doubt, I need a Higher Power's help to stay on this royal highway. If I proceed without H.P., my mind will return to rambling—dragging me back into a shameful pit of obsession and addiction.

Sayings of the Sages

Seek good and not evil so that you may live.
    —*Amos 5:14*

The mind . . . can be controlled . . . by constant practice and non-attachment.
    —*Bhagavad Gita VI, 35*

A Hunk of Healing Humor

The beginning is easy; what happens next is much harder.
    —*Anonymous*

Daily Affirmation

H.P. is guiding me on the road to a meaningful life.

Twelve Step Thought

In practicing the Fourth Step over time, I gradually grew more morally conscious. As I catalogued my negative and selfish habits, I resurrected my deadened conscience. Just trying to imitate others isn't sufficient. After all, I'm different from others in some ways. Yet, like others, I harbor some inherent moral obligations which must be met for my soul to reach a peaceful state. Slowly but surely, I began to understand what being a "good" person meant for me. Essential to this process are discovering my real self and being true to my Self. Being moral cannot involve telling stories about how I might have been. Rather, I need to see clearly how I am.

Sayings of the Sages

And, seeing their faith, Jesus said to the paralytic: "Child, your sins are forgiven."
　　　—*Mark 2:5*

A large part of people's time is spent in thinking and acting just like other people, while at the same time they energetically claim that they are "different."
　　　—*Idries Shah, Reflections*

A Hunk of Healing Humor

I am always at a loss to know how much to believe of my own stories.
　　　—*Washington Irving*

Daily Affirmation

Today, I'm being true to my Self.

Twelve Step Thought

Making a searching and fearless moral inventory allows me to live much more consciously. For me, recovery is being fully aware. There's no longer any need for me to "stuff" knowledge at a subconscious level. So I'm now living creatively instead of being pathologically dependent. At bottom, unconscious people are simply reactive; conscious people are proactive. I choose to remain awake to the exciting spiritual reality that I've discovered. With wide-open eyes, I'm actively bearing the yoke connecting me with my Higher Power. I'm finally becoming liberated from the sick sleep that characterized my former obsession. Thanks to H.P., I'm conscious and free.

Sayings of the Sages

Follow then the shining ones, the wise, the awakened, the loving.
    —*Dhammapada, 15*

Night for others is day for the disciplined soul; and day for others is night for the sage of vision.
    —*Bhagavad Gita II, 69*

A Hunk of Healing Humor

Morality is simply the attitude we adopt toward people we personally dislike.
    —*Oscar Wilde*

Daily Affirmation

My Higher Power is making me conscious and free.

APRIL 9

Twelve Step Thought

In elaborating on my moral inventory, I discovered that I had tremendous control needs. And I used many methods of controlling others. At times, I dominated the persons closest to me through covert manipulation; other times, I controlled people by becoming overly dependent on them. The solution lies in letting go. To do so, I have to work on changing some of my behaviors. Newfound friends in recovery suggested that I live the First Step more in depth—realizing that I'm truly powerless over people, places, things, and that my life is indeed unmanageable. In this process, I found that I could adjust to some self-discipline and that I could somewhat shape my life to existing conditions.

Sayings of the Sages

The Lord has made all things for Himself. A man's heart plans his way, but the Lord directs his steps.
    —*Proverbs 16:4 & 9*

I am the vine; you are the branches. If a man remains in me and I in him, he will bear much fruit; apart from me you can do nothing.
    —*John 15:5*

A Hunk of Healing Humor

There are two tragedies in life. One is not to get your heart's desire. The other is to get it.
    —*George Bernard Shaw*

Daily Affirmation

I'm powerless over people, places, and things.

Twelve Step Thought

Some years into recovery, I took the time to look over the quality of my doings. For me, morally "good" action is that which leads to man's attainment of his ultimate end. I happen to believe that the goal of human beings is eternal happiness in union with the Supreme Being. So the purpose of my existence is already fixed. My choices are solely concerned with the means to achieve my final end. In this sense, within certain basic moral parameters, the end justifies the means. I must choose the path I'll walk. And I want to use methods which achieve constant conscious contact with H.P.

Sayings of the Sages

For blessedness lieth not in much and many, but in One and oneness. It lieth alone in God and in his works. Therefore I must wait only on God and his work, and leave on one side all creatures with their works, and first of all myself.

—*Theologia Germanica, IX*

A Hunk of Healing Humor

The intelligent man finds almost everything ridiculous.

—*Goethe*

Daily Affirmation

I'm seeking constant conscious contact with my Higher Power.

Twelve Step Thought

I reviewed my weaknesses and my strengths. I found that pride is the major obstacle to my really making any progress. Prior to this evaluation, I practiced a lot of self-justification. For a number of inane reasons, I was intent on keeping my shaky pride from suffering any humiliation. Such is the route of an ego operating apart from its Higher Power. Always, it's this negative ego that gets in my way. In fact, it had been dragging me deeper and deeper into the quicksand of obsession and addiction. Now, I'm seeking that positive ego which works so closely with the ennobling ocean of spiritual energy that underlies all reality.

Sayings of the Sages

Avert my eyes from lingering on inanities, give me life in your path.
    —*Psalm 119:37*

The humble is the root of the noble.
    —*Tao Te Ching, 39*

A Hunk of Healing Humor

To be a man's own fool is bad enough; but the vain man is everybody's.
    —*William Penn*

Daily Affirmation

My positive ego is operating on spiritual energy.

Twelve Step Thought

Addictive and emotionally unstable people are prone to extremes of behavior. Personally, I know that writing a careful inventory revealed traits on totally opposite ends of the scale. I was filled with so much guilt, self-loathing, and despair that suicide seemed a possible solution. On the other end of the spectrum, I had exhibited self-righteousness, grandiosity, and self-justification. My illness somehow incorporated vast polarities. Graced by some spiritual energy, I've become much less an extremist. In fact, on a very practical basis, I'm finding that practicing moderation in all things leads to peace of soul.

Sayings of the Sages

A well developed sense of the dramatic has values beyond what people usually imagine. One of these is to realize the limitations of a sense of the dramatic.
    —Idries Shah, Reflections

You must not say, "This is worse than that," for everything will prove its value in time.
    —Ecclesiasticus 39:39 & 40

A Hunk of Healing Humor

If you talk to God, you are praying; if God talks to you, you have schizophrenia.
    —Thomas Szasz, M.D.

Daily Affirmation

Today, I'm practicing moderation in all things.

Twelve Step Thought

Old-timers in recovery told me that a true inventory lists positive as well as negative points. I did find that I possessed some assets which could be noted along with my liabilities. Of course, I felt badly about all the crazy behavior which I had inflicted on people around me. Yet, I now more readily appreciate those "good" qualities which have continued to develop and which make life simpler for persons around me. So, without succumbing again to addiction, I'm learning to live as a child of this earth whose spirit longs to soar. The bad news is that this whole growth process takes time. The good news is that my Higher Power is helping me free that spirit.

Sayings of the Sages

The kingdom of God is near. Repent and live the good news.
—*Mark 1:15*

The great earth burdens me with a body, causes me to toil in life, eases me in old age, and rests me in death. That which makes my life good, makes my death good also.
—*Chuang Tsu: Inner Chapters, 6*

A Hunk of Healing Humor

There is a thin line between genius and insanity. I have erased this line.
—*Oscar Levant*

Daily Affirmation

Thanks to H.P., my spirit is becoming free.

Twelve Step Thought

I learned the hard way that recovering doesn't exist without willingness, honesty, and open-mindedness. These are the indispensable essentials of my recovery. Willingness tunes me in to accepting my fate on this planet. Honesty is admitting my faults (as well as my strengths) and my feelings about myself. Open-mindedness is the active quietness that helps me really hear what others are saying. These are the preconditions to my becoming whole and spiritually sane—with a Higher Power guiding my growth.

Sayings of the Sages

If we claim to be without sin, we deceive ourselves.
  —*I John 1:8*

Let us throw off everything that hinders and the sin that so easily entangles, and let us run with perseverance the race marked out for us.
  —*Hebrews 12:1*

A Hunk of Healing Humor

I generally avoid temptation unless I can't resist it.
  —*Mae West*

Daily Affirmation

A Higher Power is guiding my personal growth.

Twelve Step Thought

Unless I pursue self-assessment, I'm setting myself up for discontentment and failure in recovery. It takes a willing and persistent effort for me to uncover all my emotional deformities and my intellectual insecurities. And the symptoms that such flaws are still around include worry, anger, self-pity, and depression. Yet, even though I understand that I'm beset by such negative characteristics, I still find myself powerless to escape from them. So I'm turning these terrible traits over to my Higher Power. I'm asking the Spiritual Source within to release me from their grasp.

Sayings of the Sages

It is found and known of truth that a man, of himself and his own power, is nothing, hath nothing, can do and is capable of nothing but only infirmity and evil.
—*Theologia Germanica, XXVI*

Help us in this hour of crisis, the help that man can give is worthless.
—*Psalm 108:12*

A Hunk of Healing Humor

Experience enables you to recognize a mistake when you make it again.
—*Franklin P. Jones*

Daily Affirmation

The Spiritual Source within is releasing me from my negative characteristics.

Twelve Step Thought

In closely examining my feelings, I found that anger was often a smoke screen covering the sense of my own inadequacy. I had simply substituted one kind of negativity for another. I must have internalized "I'm not okay" messages somewhere along the way. It's easier to get mad rather than admit that I feel inadequate. Now, I find that my self-esteem is growing steadily. Also, I've learned that anger can be expressed appropriately in nonthreatening and nonabusive ways. Then, I can let go of being angry along with accepting myself as adequate.

Sayings of the Sages

Control the senses from the beginning and slay this sinful destroyer of wisdom and discrimination.
    —*Bhagavad Gita III, 41*

The sage is sharp but not cutting.
    —*Tao Te Ching, 58*

A Hunk of Healing Humor

Never go to bed mad. Stay up and fight.
    —*Phyllis Diller*

Daily Affirmation

Today, I let go of anger and accept me as worthy.

Twelve Step Thought

One definition of *resentment* is a state of active mental addictiveness. When I'm holding on to anger against another individual, I definitely am resenting that person. In fact, I'm refusing to forgive that person for whatever injustice I perceived her/him doing to me. I even refused to see how hanging on to a particular irateness was really a manifestation of my own deep-rooted fears. That is when I most need to trust my Higher Power. It took a while to realize and accept that *resentment* destroys more addicted persons than anything else.

Sayings of the Sages

If you forgive men when they sin against you, your heavenly father will also forgive you.
    —*Matthew 6:14*

Empty yourself of everything. Let the mind rest at peace.
    —*Tao Te Ching, 16*

A Hunk of Healing Humor

I never take my own side in a quarrel.
    —*Robert Frost*

Daily Affirmation

Today, I'm faking forgiveness until I make it a habit.

Twelve Step Thought

In getting to the bottom of my anger, I'm finding that I more easily accept others doing things differently than me. In fact, Twelve Step Programs teach that the practice of tolerance is a necessary part of recovery. At times, it's true—I tolerate the irritating behavior of some people. On a few occasions, I've come very close to screaming swear words at someone or to verbally kicking a person in a quite sensitive spot. Fortunately, I ask my Higher Power for help when so tempted. Sometimes, my being tolerant is increased understanding; other times, it's simply an urgent prayer.

Sayings of the Sages

Though princes put me on trial, your servant will meditate on your statutes.
    —*Psalm 119:23*

The sage keeps his knowledge to himself while ordinary men flaunt their knowledge in loud discussion. So I say, "Those who dispute do not see."
    —*Chuang Tsu: Inner Chapters, 2*

A Hunk of Healing Humor

I do desire we may be better strangers.
    —*William Shakespeare*

Daily Affirmation

I'm practicing tolerance today—with H.P.'s help.

Twelve Step Thought

Blaming others was a great way out for explaining the unusual difficulties in my life. It's truly a convenient escape hatch. If you-know-who was to blame, then yours-truly was off the hook. I learned the hard way that this scapegoating combines both denial and avoidance of responsibility. It allowed my addiction to drag on for a long time—slowly wasting my body and my mind. Finally, this poisonous combination brought me close enough to death's door for me to seek help. I realized this was *my* dilemma. I started to stop blaming others. I needed to for my very survival. And I trusted a Higher Power to save me.

Sayings of the Sages

Look to your own faults, what you have done or left undone. Overlook the faults of others.
    —*Dhammapada, 4*

Stop judging by mere appearances, and make a right judgment.
    —*John 7:24*

A Hunk of Healing Humor

There are two reasons for doing things—a very good reason and the real reason.
    —*Anonymous*

Daily Affirmation

I'm being honest about me, and not blaming others.

Twelve Step Thought

A number of us in recovery have discovered that professional help often can ensure a solid start on a Fourth Step. In short, many need all the support they can get to be restored to sanity. Sometimes, a highly regarded counseling psychologist facilitates the finding of paths leading to freedom. In fact, some individuals simply cannot escape their obsessive fears without the special input of a competent counselor. After all, getting better takes what it takes. An honest Third Step and appropriate psychotherapy go hand in hand. They lead inevitably to a searching and fearless moral inventory.

Sayings of the Sages

Give to Caesar what is Caesar's, and to God what is God's.
—*Matthew 22:21*

Knowing ignorance is strength. Ignoring knowledge is sickness.
—*Tao Te Ching, 71*

A Hunk of Healing Humor

As scarce as truth is, the supply has always been in excess of the demand.
—*Josh Billings*

Daily Affirmation

It's okay to ask for help when I'm seeking truth.

Twelve Step Thought

For many months into recovery, I grasped any available excuse for avoiding an inventory of myself. Blaming others was often a convenient way out. Over time, I came to understand the gravity of my situation. Right action became absolutely necessary to avoid further disaster. When I'm noticeably disturbed, my *foremost* need is for quieting the disturbance—regardless of who or what *I thought* might have caused it. Thus, for me, a written self-evaluation could make the difference between being in recovery and launching another addictive episode.

Sayings of the Sages

Denial and affirmation are games which people play. There are people who deny that they are capable of denying, and who would insist that people do not insist.
    —*Idries Shah, Reflections*

By what is a man impelled to commit sin, as if by force, even against his will . . . ?
    —*Bhagavad Gita III, 36*

A Hunk of Healing Humor

If you don't now where you are going, you may end up someplace else.
    —*Laurence J. Peter*

Daily Affirmation

I'm pursuing honest self-assessment and right action.

Twelve Step Thought

My life now is fairly focused on finding a higher level of consciousness. But, for a long time, I thought that I was in control of my life. Being me was very mechanical—like driving an automobile. I would race here and there at ever-higher speeds without having the slightest idea of where the heck I was going. And the roads were getting bumpier as well as full of potholes. The thrill of driving was being transformed into some terrible silent fear. I needed to slow down and figure out where I wanted to go. To do so, I found that I must step on the brake and get out of the driver's seat. Only then could I appropriately inspect my addictive personality.

Sayings of the Sages

Relieve the distress of my heart, free me from my sufferings.
　　　—*Psalm 25:17*

One can only know things through knowing oneself.
　　　—*Chuang Tsu: Inner Chapters, 2*

A Hunk of Healing Humor

There is a great deal of human nature in people.
　　　—*Mark Twain*

Daily Affirmation

Today, I'm getting to know myself better.

Twelve Step Thought

For many years, I almost never analyzed my actions. Because I moved about blindly, having little understanding of my motivations, I often imposed myself unreasonably upon others. Sometimes, I left a long trail of unhappiness behind me. Yet, rather than wait for punishment in an afterlife, it seems that I paid (and am still paying) the price of my mistakes all along the way. When I finally wrote out the lows and the highs of my life, I was truly sorry for the hurt caused to others. I was open to amends. I accepted that, for the scales of justice/karma to balance out, I would be called on again by H.P. to pass more than one acid test.

Sayings of the Sages

All law-breaking is like a two-edged sword.
     —*Ecclesiasticus 21:4*

Speak or act with an impure mind and trouble will follow you ... Speak or act with a pure mind and happiness will follow you.
     —*Dhammapada, 1*

A Hunk of Healing Humor

Most people repent their sins by thanking God they ain't so wicked as their neighbors.
     —*Josh Billings*

Daily Affirmation

My Higher Power helps me accept the balancing out of my misdeeds.

Twelve Step Thought

Cultivating an honest and realistic approach to who and what I am is essential to the maintenance of my recovery. To do this, I have to elaborate periodically on my initial Fourth Step—reviewing what addiction can do to me. This process serves as a kind of partial or term insurance against a possible return to active addictiveness (the "yets" talked about at meetings). On my "shadow" side, a belligerent beast is locked securely in the psychic basement of my being. Yet, in a sense, my addict ways are always breaking out somehow. For now, I can review my status in my personal journal; and I can seek my Higher Power's help to keep moving.

Sayings of the Sages

One should not give up the work suited to one's nature . . . though it may be defective, for all enterprises are clouded by defects as fire by smoke.
  —*Bhagavad Gita XVIII, 48*

Whatsoever makes the wavering and unsteady mind wander away, let him restrain and bring it back to the control of the Self alone.
  —*Bhagavad Gita VI, 26*

A Hunk of Healing Humor

The pure and simple truth is rarely pure and never simple.
  —*Oscar Wilde*

Daily Affirmation

My Higher Power helps me to see where I am and to keep moving.

Twelve Step Thought

In-depth assessments have convinced me that my personality is tinged indelibly with multifaceted addictiveness. Inside me, there's an all-pervasive obsessiveness that seems to transfer from one form into another. First, I was overly dependent on other persons. Then, I was sexually addicted—especially in using indiscriminate sex as a means of relieving my frustrations. Later, I manifested addiction to alcohol and other drugs. In leaving the bottle and various substances behind, I was left with the nicotine monkey on my back. Now, I find that I'm orally fixated on certain foods. So, once again, I'm seeking a solution through a Higher Power.

Sayings of the Sages

To keep me from becoming conceited ... there was given me a thorn in my flesh. The Lord said to me, "My grace is sufficient ... for my power is made perfect in weakness."
    —*II Corinthians 12:7 & 9*

Like a fish out of water, stranded on the shore, thoughts thrash and quiver. For how can they shake off desire?
    —*Dhammapada, 3*

A Hunk of Healing Humor

Her personality is as false as her teeth.
    —*Anonymous*

Daily Affirmation

Today, a Higher Power is delivering me from obsessions.

Twelve Step Thought

Step Four is a kind of spiritual spring cleaning for my soul. All the unused corners which are strung with cobwebs get wiped down and renewed. It's actually shocking to see a dust-laden mirror reflecting the light of truth upon being dusted. This thorough housecleaning reveals realities that I had purposefully forgotten. So items once pushed back out of awareness now are brought forward to be dealt with. In fact, doing a Fourth is getting honest about all my affairs—clearly expressing a personal performance review in writing.

Sayings of the Sages

God, . . . probe me and know my thoughts.
—*Psalm 139:23*

He uses his knowledge to perfect his mind and he uses his mind to attain the universal mind.
—*Chuang Tsu: Inner Chapters, 5*

A Hunk of Healing Humor

Be yourself. Who else is better qualified?
—*Frank J. Giblin, Jr.*

Daily Affirmation

I'm using self-knowledge to perfect my mind.

Twelve Step Thought

When I was worrying too much, I was only working half a program. This realization came to me while I was doing a Fourth Step. For me, a *laissez-faire* attitude toward people, places, and things actually rattles my chained obsessive/compulsive monster—reminding me it's there, seeking to be loosed and to become active once more. I must carefully avoid unwarranted worries as if I were avoiding the plague. The solution lies in implementing a plan of personal growth. My methods for doing so are found in the guidelines of anonymous Twelve Step Programs. And related healing feedback is as close as my therapist. When I do the "footwork," H.P. lifts the weight of all worries from me.

Sayings of the Sages

People usually fail when they are on the verge of success. So give as much care to the end as to the beginning; then there will be no failure.
　　—Tao Te Ching, 64

You need to persevere so that, when you have done the will of God, you will receive what he has promised.
　　—Hebrews 10:36

A Hunk of Healing Humor

Sometimes I act pretty stupid, just so people will accept me as an equal.
　　—William Roylance

Daily Affirmation

My Higher Power is relieving me of all worries.

Twelve Step Thought

Not to worry about forgetting something on your inventory! It's better not to procrastinate. Many, including myself, found relief in mentally reserving space for blind spots which would be uncovered later. As the Johari Window exercise demonstrates, there's an area of each individual not known to oneself but indeed known to others. Of course, the Johari Window is a graphic model of awareness in *interpersonal* relations. However, one can visualize the increase in self-knowledge as a similar ongoing process of revelation. The saying "More shall be revealed" pertains to everyone engaged in a program of personal growth.

Sayings of the Sages

Direct my steps as you have promised, let evil win no power over me.
    —*Psalm 119:133*

Where a creature or a man forsaketh and cometh out of himself and his own things, there God entereth in with His own, that is, with Himself.
    —*Theologia Germanica, XXIV*

A Hunk of Healing Humor

When three people call you an ass, put on a bridle.
    —*Spanish proverb*

Daily Affirmation

More shall be revealed!

Twelve Step Thought

Getting honest with myself required that I reveal to a kindred spirit all the dark secrets which I had stuffed deep down in my gut. With much trepidation, I finally shared those fearful and guilt-ridden aspects of my being which I had walled off from all who knew me. Through some miracle, I bypassed my ego's lying grandiosity. Finding peace was more important. And I felt much lighter when I opened up and shared the reality of my sorrows and my joys.

Sayings of the Sages

The seeker, who has put away sin, experiences easily the infinite bliss of contact with the Eternal.
   —*Bhagavad Gita VI, 28*

Do what you have to do resolutely, with all your heart.
   —*Dhammapada, 22*

A Hunk of Healing Humor

I talk to myself because I like dealing with a better class of people.
   —*Jackie Mason*

Daily Affirmation

Honesty gives me peace of mind.

Twelve Step Thought

Sharing my story with another helped me to stop living in the past. Bit by bit, I realized that my moments of calm and contentment depend on self-honesty and on living *today*. My rampaging obsession remains, but only as a monster chained in a dungeon of yesterday. Admitting my misdeeds to my Higher Power *and* to a fellow human being greatly freed me from the tyranny and fear of bygone days. For me, peace and happiness are found in the eternal now.

Sayings of the Sages

History is not usually what has happened. History is what some people have thought to be significant.
　　—Idries Shah, Reflections

Enveloped is wisdom by this insatiable fire of desire, which is the constant foe of the wise.
　　—Bhagavad Gita III, 39

A Hunk of Healing Humor

The man who thinks he has no faults has at least one.
　　—Herbert Prochnow

Daily Affirmation

I am totally focused on today.

Twelve Step Thought

After I shared my whole story with a fellow Twelve Stepper, I was relieved of the entire burden of guilt from my past. I finally came to live in today. I began to experience the reality of "now." I gradually perceived the meaning of living in the moment. I saw that "now" is not a noun. "Now" is being in process. "Now" is total consciousness of awareness. In truth, "now" is indescribable. If anything, in its ever-fleeting activeness, "now" is a verb. And, upon admitting the exact nature of my wrongs to a sponsor, I was blessed for a while with immersion in each instant.

Sayings of the Sages

There is a season for everything, a time for every occupation under heaven.
—*Ecclesiastes 3:1*

Having transcended the distinction of past and present, he began to enter the land where there is no life or death, where killing does not take away life and giving birth does not add to it.
—*Chuang Tsu: Inner Chapters, 6*

A Hunk of Healing Humor

I may have faults but being wrong ain't one of them.
—*Jimmy Hoffa*

Daily Affirmation

I'm immersed in this instant.

Twelve Step Thought

It was with great fear and trepidation that I first approached revealing the intimacies of my life to another human being. I stated emphatically that I now recognized what my problems were. God knew already. The Divinity knows all. So why involve anyone else? Yet Step Five insists I push beyond any natural urge and do my supernatural duty. And a definite self-restraint was involved in this deflating of my negative ego. Finally, I opted for the advice of fellow Twelve Steppers who said this step is essential for longtime sobriety and peace of mind. After I bit the bullet, I didn't feel ashamed or disgraced. Instead, I felt light and free.

Sayings of the Sages

Do not be afraid, you will not be put to shame; do not be dismayed, you will not be disgraced.
    —*Isaiah 54:4*

In caring for others and serving heaven, there is nothing like using restraint. Restraint begins with giving up one's own ideas.
    —*Tao Te Ching, 59*

A Hunk of Healing Humor

Conscience is a mother-in-law whose visit never ends.
    —*H. L. Mencken*

Daily Affirmation

Today, I feel light and free.

Twelve Step Thought

Upon telling my tale of wrongs (many) and rights (few), I definitely experienced the simple fact that confession is good for the soul. Yet, it hadn't been easy to select and ask someone to hear my story. I chose a sponsor who patiently listened to my list of fears and faults, and who shared some equally devastating character defects. Then this sponsor welcomed me to a whole new level of spiritual kinship. Now, I understand that I was loved as a fellow seeker. I've discovered that, besides God and my personal partner, another person could love me in my weakness.

Sayings of the Sages

In my inner being, I delight in God's law; but I see another law at work in the members of my body, waging war against the law of my mind. ... Who will rescue me from this body of death?
　　—*Romans 7:22–24*

Whatever you do, work at it with all your heart, as working for the Lord.
　　—*Colossians 3:23*

A Hunk of Healing Humor

Never exaggerate your faults; your friends will attend to that.
　　—*Robert C. Edwards*

Daily Affirmation

Today, I delight in God's love.

Twelve Step Thought

Before I could begin mining the Twelve Steps, I had to feel that it was okay to be in recovery. Much later on, I realized that I had found unconditional love in self-help meetings. The only real requirement for inclusion was the desire to become recovered. And being in such a group felt so safe. So I no longer had to isolate myself. There were others around who were very much like me in their compulsiveness. Ultimately, it was this same sense of okayness and the atmosphere of trust that provided me with the support necessary for admitting my wrongs to another human.

Sayings of the Sages

Flow with whatever may happen and let your mind be free.
—*Chuang Tsu: Inner Chapters, 4*

To "see both sides" of a problem is the surest way to prevent its complete solution. Because there are always more than two sides.
—*Idries Shah, Reflections*

A Hunk of Healing Humor

Some of us are like wheelbarrows—only useful when pushed, and very easily upset.
—*Jack Herbert*

Daily Affirmation

Today, I'm experiencing unconditional love.

MAY 7

Twelve Step Thought

Holding back on total self-revelation to a trustworthy person is the sign of a severely maladjusted attitude. An acquaintance of mine trudged around in this precarious position for eleven years. The strain must have been tremendous. (He only talked about it after the fact.) Then, one sunny day, he just "cracked up." He entered a whirlwind of active addiction. Within a matter of months, he seemed to age ten years. Fortunately, he made it back to recovering status. Yet, he paid a very high price for waiting so hellishly long to pull the last secrets from his "gut." So share it all. Beware sick old-timers. Pray for their release. Be open.

Sayings of the Sages

Where False Light is, there men become heedless of Christ's life and all virtue.
—*Theologia Germanica, XL*

How easy it is to see your brother's faults, how hard to face your own. You winnow his in the wind like chaff, but yours you hide, like a cheat covering up an unlucky throw.
—*Dhammapada, 18*

A Hunk of Healing Humor

By trying we can easily learn to endure adversity—another man's I mean.
—*Mark Twain*

Daily Affirmation

I'm no longer keeping any secrets.

Twelve Step Thought

Fearlessly admitting my defects to another person miraculously wrapped me in the merciful cocoon of divine grace. I even had the feeling that there must be rejoicing in some spiritual realm over my fully declared repentance. On the very brink of my personal doom, I found forgiveness and relief. Yet, how easy it is to forget my weakness! For me to remain recovering, I simply cannot risk living complacently. Not giving in to my destructive obsessions requires an ongoing reliance on my Inner Guide, my Higher Power. I continue to admit how weak my little ego is. H.P. carries me across the fearful void of existence.

Sayings of the Sages

There is more rejoicing in heaven over one sinner who repents than over ninety-nine just persons who do not need to repent.
    —*Luke 15:7*

The Way is the support of the myriad creatures. It is the protection of the good man, and the refuge of the bad.
    —*Tao Te Ching, 62*

A Hunk of Healing Humor

Never look behind you. Something may be gaining on you.
    —*Satchel Paige*

Daily Affirmation

My Higher Power is showing me the right path.

Twelve Step Thought

Upon conscientiously admitting my wrongs to God and myself and another human being, I felt washed clean of my guilt and blessed with a new freedom of spirit. Feelings of shame and unworthiness were in process of being detached from my central self. These huge emotional millstones would no longer drag me relentlessly down into the depths of despair. Rather, my Higher Power's grace-laden goodness snapped the anchor chain from around my neck. Now, I can stand tall among my brothers and sisters without constantly having to glance over my shoulder. For the first time in my life, I can look the world in the eye.

Sayings of the Sages

Have mercy on me, O God, in your goodness, in your great tenderness wipe away my faults; wash me clean of my guilt, purify me from my sin.
  —*Psalm 51:1 & 2*

He who knows Me, the unborn, without beginning, also the mighty lord of the worlds, he, among mortals is undeluded and freed from all sins.
  —*Bhagavad Gita X, 3*

A Hunk of Healing Humor

I do have many faults, but I'm divorcing them.
  —*William Roylance*

Daily Affirmation

I'm worthy of standing tall today.

Twelve Step Thought

A spiritual advisor once told me that I need to immediately face whatever makes me feel uncomfortable. Unreservedly telling the tale of my misdeeds to another sure fits with that advice. To tell the truth is relatively simple, but it's not so easy. Facing up to the sordidness of my past caused me much anxiety. And, yet, sincere willingness and some movement were enough. I had barely taken a few steps in the right direction when God's compassionate energy gathered me up and carried me the rest of the way. After being lost for so long, I found that the mere intention of pursuing atonement through confession sufficed to provide me with a sense of oneness with all that is.

Sayings of the Sages

While he was still a long way off, his father saw him and was filled with compassion for him. ... This son of mine was dead and is alive again; he was lost and is found.
       —*Luke 15:20 & 24*

He who loses the way feels lost. When you are at one with the Tao, the Tao welcomes you.
       —*Tao Te Ching, 23*

A Hunk of Healing Humor

The average person thinks he isn't.
       —*Father Larry Lorenzoni*

Daily Affirmation

Spiritual energy supports me in all that I do.

Twelve Step Thought

Truthfully, I never did find any real relief in confessing the sins of other people. Yet, I often found it easy to take someone else's inventory. That practice sufficed for a while. Still, deep in my center, I knew that a different sort of declaration was needed. At last, I came to realize consciously that I needed to tell my own story. Screwing up my courage and praying earnestly, I set out to reveal my tale. Surprise! My parable of being lost paralleled others which I had read and heard about. And, upon sharing all, the greatest revelation was my feeling of unity with everyone I had so readily criticized.

Sayings of the Sages

I am the gate; whoever enters through me will be saved.
—*John 10:9*

Those who justify their faults to avoid punishment are many, and those who do not justify their faults and refuse to be spared are few. But only the virtuous man can resign himself to the inevitable and accept it as fate.
—*Chuang Tsu: Inner Chapters, 5*

A Hunk of Healing Humor

I feel bad that I don't feel worse.
—*Michael Frayn*

Daily Affirmation

I'm feeling a oneness with everyone I meet today.

Twelve Step Thought

Once I sincerely shared where I'm at and where I've been, a doorway to freedom appeared. No longer did I feel so terribly lonely. Neither did I feel so compelled to isolate myself. I let go of being guiltily walled in by the ghosts of yesterday. What a wonderful benefit! No longer imprisoned in that negative mindcage, I was graced with being rid of a crushing sense of isolation. So I've tasted the truth that I no longer have to be totally alone. And, indeed, some fellow seekers are now my friends.

Sayings of the Sages

When anyone says "*I* am beyond *that*," you may be sure that *it* is beyond *him*. Not because it must be beyond him, but because if he were beyond it, he would not say it.
        —*Idries Shah, Reflections*

Let us hold fast the confession of our hope without wavering, for he who promised is faithful.
        —*Hebrews 10:23*

A Hunk of Healing Humor

Man is the only animal that blushes. Or needs to.
        —*Mark Twain*

Daily Affirmation

I'm no longer alone.

Twelve Step Thought

Sure, I believed that God could forgive my many mistakes. However, I needed another human being to witness my admission. Hadn't I spent much of my life fooling myself? Without the more objective help of a trusted fellow, how could I really be sure that I wasn't still self-deceived? Certainly, lack of honesty was one of my outstanding character faults. As a matter of fact, I had bragged about being one of the great B.S. artists of the twentieth century. So my confession required assistance from outside myself. I found a recovering person who could understand my story and keep me honest.

Sayings of the Sages

Who can forgive sins but God alone?
      —*Mark 2:7*

Speak the truth. Give whatever you can. Never be angry. These three steps will lead you into the presence of the gods.
      —*Dhammapada, 17*

A Hunk of Healing Humor

Whenever I'm caught between two evils, I take the one I've never tried.
      —*Mae West*

Daily Affirmation

Today, I'm speaking the truth.

Twelve Step Thought

Other people keep me honest. I mean those in the same spiritual program of recovery. Without doubt, at any given time I am "disobeying" or ignoring some of the Twelve Steps. But I try not to lie about this at meetings. It's hard to con a fellow con artist—especially when she or he has already lived through whatever predicament I'm in now. Besides, I don't really have to say anything. More experienced members can (and do) read my facial expression and my body language. Then, they send up a few trial balloons. Depending on my reaction, they bless me with the most appropriate Program advice. So I'm forced to be truthful in my sharing.

Sayings of the Sages

If we claim to be without sin, we deceive ourselves and the truth is not in us.
    —*I John 1:8*

Disobedience and sin are the same thing, for there is no sin but disobedience, and what is done of disobedience is all sin. Therefore all we have to do is keep ourselves from disobedience.
    —*Theologia Germanica, XVI*

A Hunk of Healing Humor

You're supposed to accept everything I say as the truth—until I change my mind.
    —*William Roylance*

Daily Affirmation

Today, I'm in tune with the Twelve Steps.

Twelve Step Thought

In addition to holding back nothing in the sharing of my personal inventory, it was strongly suggested that I should develop a willingness to take advice and to accept direction. I was informed that only after taking such measures would I begin to experience clear thinking, solid honesty, and genuine humility. For me, this meant talking more frequently with my sponsor. Also, it involved letting go of my negative ego's separate will. This meant meditating more often, as regular meditation makes it easier for me to let go, to give up my need for control. Today I'm willing to listen and to accept suggestions.

Sayings of the Sages

Submit to such as these and to everyone who joins in the work and labors at it.
   —*I Corinthians 16:16*

I will declare to thee in full this wisdom together with knowledge by knowing which there shall remain nothing more here left to know.
   —*Bhagavad Gita VII, 2*

A Hunk of Healing Humor

Fewer things are harder to put up with than the annoyance of a good example.
   —*Mark Twain*

Daily Affirmation

I'm following my sponsor's suggestions.

Twelve Step Thought

After I carried out this step with all possible humility, I instinctively knew deep inside that I had done the right thing. In fact, in honestly going through this confessional process, I surely trusted my Higher Power. And I found a similar experience in pursuing each of the Twelve Steps. For me, there is a right way to approach and engage these principles of recovery. When I savor the Steps in my self-appropriate manner, I feel very peaceful. Yet, I must ascertain that what I do is indeed right for me. I cannot blindly imitate others. I need my own internal balance. For me, rightly practiced, the Steps lead to emotional equilibrium.

Sayings of the Sages

Do not let your hearts be troubled. Trust in God.
    —*John 14:1*

Surrender yourself humbly; then you can be trusted to care for all things. Love the world as your own self; then you can truly care for all things.
    —*Tao Te Ching, 13*

A Hunk of Healing Humor

Honesty is the best policy—when there is money in it.
    —*Mark Twain*

Daily Affirmation

The Steps are giving me emotional balance.

Twelve Step Thought

As I more frequently turned my will and my life over to the care of my Higher Power, I was graced with a basic level of humility. Then, I clearly saw the tenuous nature of my situation: left to itself, my negative ego would utterly destroy me. There's little consolation for me in human terms. To some, I'm the victim of an insidious disease or a behavioral abberation; to others, I'm a moral weakling or an outright sinner. I'm viewed according to my compulsive labels. Yet, in my very weakness lies the greatest hope for my salvation. I've been reduced to calling on God for the strength to live each day.

Sayings of the Sages

We were under great pressure, far beyond our ability to endure. ... But this happened that we might not rely on ourselves but on God.
    —*II Corinthians 1:8 & 9*

If the whole world praised him he would not be moved. If the whole world blamed him he would not be discouraged.
    —*Chuang Tsu: Inner Chapters, 1*

A Hunk of Healing Humor

We all have flaws, and mine is being wicked.
    —*James Thurber*

Daily Affirmation

God is the strength in my day.

Twelve Step Thought

Thanks to grace, I became honest enough to have the recitation of my wrongs witnessed by a fellow Twelve Stepper. But what animated this admission was a heartbreaking cry *de profundis*, wherein my soul's voice shouted out the peculiarities of my sordid state to the All-Merciful One. And, in this childlike act of faith, I inevitably recognized the Almighty as the Source of my existence. So I came to believe that there's a divine spark (however small) burning in my breast. That explains the insatiable yearning which flares forth intermittently from the depths of my being! The pull of this Firegod's gravitational field draws me relentlessly toward reunion.

Sayings of the Sages

From the depths I call to you . . . Lord, listen to my cry for help. I wait for the Lord, my soul waits for him.
　　—*Psalm 130:1, 2, 5*

This was the true light that gives light to every man who comes into the world.
　　—*John 1:9*

A Hunk of Healing Humor

I've developed a new philosophy—I only dread one day at a time.
　　—*Charles M. Schulz*

Daily Affirmation

There's a divine spark burning in me.

Twelve Step Thought

Sometime after completing my confession, I was able to thank the Eternal Lover for the gift of suffering. Finally, I could admit that pain was part of my reality. After all, it was the huge hurt of my addiction that had truly brought me to my knees. And hurting brought me closer to my Higher Power ongoingly. While I was in a meditative state one day, I was transported to a wall-less room filled with light, which I had only glimpsed before when I was "high." Even given the cares and griefs that encircle my life, I could be blessed with transcendence. I realized my life objective is to dwell in that lightful room.

Sayings of the Sages

Now the dwelling of God is with man, and he will live with them.
   —*Revelation 21:3*

The light shines in the darkness, and the darkness has not overcome it.
   —*John 1:5*

A Hunk of Healing Humor

If you pick up a starving dog and make him prosperous, he will not bite you. This is the principal difference between a dog and a man.
   —*Mark Twain*

Daily Affirmation

My Higher Power is helping me to transcend pain.

Twelve Step Thought

All the Steps seem to flow together when I'm seriously working my program. I suspect that, to unreservedly practice each principle, one must be engaged somehow in the eleven others. Anyway, I do the footwork to the best of my ability. Any moments of ecstasy (unlike hallucinations) are gifts from above. I'm attempting to become the highest I can be. Based on my Higher Power's strength, I strive for communion with that which is spiritual. Deep in my soul, I know the possibility of constant conscious contact with the Beloved. And suffering felt on one level turns into bliss at the portal of a whole other dimension where I'm held in holy arms.

Sayings of the Sages

He has come to the end of the way. All that he had to do, he has done. And now he is one.
　　—Dhammapada, 26

Without attachment, perform always the work that has to be done.
　　—Bhagavad Gita III, 19

A Hunk of Healing Humor

Virtue must be valuable, if men and women of all degrees pretend to have it.
　　—Ed Howe

Daily Affirmation

Today, I'm united with that which is spiritual.

Twelve Step Thought

Today, I walk my path with more humility. My trek is like the famous "Footprints" story. At the lowest points in my life, only one set of footprints appeared across the sands of time. In working a Fourth and Fifth Step, my hurt ego cried, "Where were you, Lord, then?" For a while, I got mighty angry at God. I accused: "When I needed you the most, you left my side." Then, in the silent listening of my meditation, an answer came through from the Source of light and love: "Sweet soul, I've always been with you. During your greatest trials and sufferings, in which you felt alone and saw but one set of footprints, it was then I carried you."

Sayings of the Sages

Out of compassion for those devoted ones, remaining within my own true state, I destroy the darkness born of ignorance by the shining lamp of wisdom.
    —*Bhagavad Gita X, 11*

Let the little children come to me . . . for the kingdom of heaven belongs to such as these.
    —*Matthew 19:14*

A Hunk of Healing Humor

Consistency requires you to be as ignorant today as you were a year ago.
    —*Bernard Berenson*

Daily Affirmation

God is carrying me through the rough spots.

Twelve Step Thought

One of my deepest desires is to become totally focused on forgiveness. For me, therein lies the key to a state of contented recovery. Forgiveness grew out of my Fifth Step. It had taken me a few attempts to resolutely and honestly tell another person the exact nature of my mistakes. Finally, when I wholeheartedly admitted my character faults, I was filled with a warm certainty that I could receive forgiveness. Also, I intuitively knew that I could forgive others (and myself as well). As I experienced the process, I discovered that to forgive is to relieve myself of a burden. Now, a step at a time, my Higher Power is guiding me to forgive in all the little incidents of life.

Sayings of the Sages

You are a God of forgiveness, gracious and loving.
   —*Nehemiah 9:17*

Forgive, and you will be forgiven.
   —*Luke 6:37*

A Hunk of Healing Humor

Moral indignation is jealousy with a halo.
   —*H. G. Wells*

Daily Affirmation

Forgiving is relieving me of a burden.

Twelve Step Thought

Everyone needs a confidant. The unburdening of one's soul takes two people. Finding someone to whom I could confide the state of my soul took a lot of careful thought. I had no best friend. I considered priests and physicians, but I had never been completely honest with any of them. Paying a therapist didn't feel right for this sort of relationship. On occasion, I shared my innermost spiritual self with a proven spiritual teacher. The outcome was good; yet, the physical presence (for confiding) was too far removed from my everyday life. Then, I was impressed by a loving and happy person at a meeting—who's now my sponsor and confidant.

Sayings of the Sages

Be assured, he who helpeth a man to his own will, helpeth him to the worst that he can. For the more a man followeth after his own self-will . . . the farther off is he from God, the true Good.
    —*Theologia Germanica, XXXIV*

Let us therefore make every effort to do what leads to peace and to mutual edification.
    —*Romans 14:19*

A Hunk of Healing Humor

Get someone else to blow your horn and the sound will carry twice as far.
    —*Will Rogers*

Daily Affirmation

Today, I'm following my sponsor's advice.

Twelve Step Thought

When the need arises, it's important that I talk with my sponsor about any unresolved conflicts in my life. Unless I take this initiative, I could let problems propel me back to the anxious and lonely feelings which characterized my life prior to recovery. I really don't want to again suffer such self-imposed isolation. I've learned this lesson in the school of hard knocks. A conflicted emotional state *requires* that one discusses it with a trusted person in order to effect any resolution at all. After I've initiated and followed through on this necessary footwork, then I'm graced with relief.

Sayings of the Sages

Sometimes breathing is hard, sometimes it comes easily;
Sometimes there is strength and sometimes weakness;
Sometimes one is up and sometimes down.
—*Tao Te Ching, 29*

Do not stand aside: trouble is near.
—*Psalm 22:11*

A Hunk of Healing Humor

I can live for two months on a good compliment.
—*Mark Twain*

Daily Affirmation

My conflicts are being resolved.

Twelve Step Thought

As part of my recovery process, I talk to God in prayer; God talks to me in meditation. And I'm basically comfortable following any advice that I receive while meditating. However, I'm not always sure about the message. Old-timers tell me this is one reason a sponsor is needed. After all, persons known for their great spirituality *insisted* on checking any supposed divine directions with their spiritual advisors. In her autobiography, Teresa of Avila is quite emphatic about this practice: "Anyone, I repeat, who surrenders his soul to a single director, and is subject to him alone, will be making a great mistake."

Sayings of the Sages

The secret of the kingdom of God has been given to you. But to those on the outside everything is said in parables.

—*Mark 4:11*

Do not look for bad company or live with men who do not care. Find friends who love the truth.

—*Dhammapada, 6*

A Hunk of Healing Humor

Fiction is obliged to stick to possibilities. Truth isn't.

—*Mark Twain*

Daily Affirmation

I look for the winners, the truth lovers.

Twelve Step Thought

For me, another advantage of having more than one sponsor is to avoid the (often unconscious) development of an overdependent relationship. In a true rehabilitative sense, recovery involves becoming a lot more independent. Even life partners can have shared independence. Becoming slavishly bound to one thing or one person or one process is the core of an addictive behavioral pattern. In the same way, I found that although conscious dependence on a Higher Power is not slavish, a Twelve Step Program couldn't be my only source of personal growth. I also found value-centered personal growth readings and yogic meditation.

Sayings of the Sages

Live in serenity and joy.
The wise man delights in the truth.
And follows the law of the awakened.
    —*Dhammapada, 6*

Continue to work out your salvation with fear and trembling, for it is God who works in you to will and do what pleases him.
    —*Philippians 2:12 & 13*

A Hunk of Healing Humor

I am not young enough to know everything.
    —*Oscar Wilde*

Daily Affirmation

I'm becoming more independent as I depend more on my Higher Power.

Twelve Step Thought

When a caterpillar changes into a butterfly, that process is called metamorphosis. A similar change can happen in recovery. Of course, this remaking is more plausible after the potential changee completes Step Five. Before, I crawled on my belly; now, at times, I can fly. I used to be a scorpion—often stinging myself. Then, I became an eaglet, seeking to soar. A self-centered and blaming animal is turning into a responsible and caring human being. For me, the true sign of a major transformation will be when I relate lovingly to others whether I'm accepted or rejected by them.

Sayings of the Sages

Do not conform any longer to the pattern of this world, but be transformed by the renewing of your mind.
—*Romans 12:2*

Once upon a time, I, Chuang Tsu, dreamed I was a butterfly flying happily here and there, enjoying life without knowing who I was.
—*Chuang Tsu: Inner Chapters, 2*

A Hunk of Healing Humor

Status quo. Latin for the mess we're in.
—*Jeve Moorman*

Daily Affirmation

Today, I'm relating lovingly to others.

Twelve Step Thought

If I can tell my inventory (albeit with much effort) to a trusted person, surely I can more often share my feelings with my soulmate. When I communicate, I want to exhibit as much fervor as I had in preparing a Fifth Step. Yes, the obstacle impeding such gut-level contact is huge. "Don't discuss how you feel!" Although injected into a child's mind, this injunction of my parent state still prevents me (forty plus years later) from sharing my feelings—even with my precious partner. I'm depending on God to solve this situation for me. There's no other recourse. I can do a daily Tenth Step on sharing myself with my special friend. Otherwise, I pray, pray, pray. . . .

Sayings of the Sages

I am my Beloved's, and my Beloved is mine.
    —*The Song of Songs 6:3*

If a man and woman . . . live together with much respect, worshipping the Lord, there will be deep joy in their family.
    —*David de Chiron*

A Hunk of Healing Humor

Marriage is really tough because you have to deal with feelings and lawyers.
    —*Richard Pryor*

Daily Affirmation

Today, I'm sharing my feelings with my partner.

Twelve Step Thought

How resistant I remain to change after some nine years of recovery! This pertains especially to my relationship with those closest to me. Redoing Step Five for newly accumulated wrongs or finally remembered old ones is a most necessary preparation for amends that I still need to make. It's much more than a follow-up on a daily inventory. It's comparable to a periodic make-up exam which catches up my grade in personal growth. Also, it naturally follows the moral inventory that I usually complete at a recovery retreat or at a weekend spiritual intensive. If effects considerable change.

Sayings of the Sages

In the Middle East one of the major blessings which is also a curse can be found in the commentaries on the teachings of spiritual masters. They are blessings for those who received them at the right time, and curses for those who ever since have struggled with them after they became anachronistic.

—*Idries Shah, Reflections*

A Hunk of Healing Humor

I believe that professional wrestling is clean and everything else in the world is fixed.

—*Frank Deford*

Daily Affirmation

I'm changing for the better.

Twelve Step Thought

I spent most of my life loaded down with guilt. No wonder I distracted myself with obsessive thoughts and compulsive actions! Like a clinging shadow, my guilt and consequent negative expectations followed me into recovery. I've finally acquired some acceptance about this fact. However limited my reaction to the situation is, I can't do more than my best on any given day. One twentieth-century preacher put it this way: "I'm not okay. You're not okay. And that's okay." As I turn more frequently to my Higher Power and to my Program footwork, the pain of guilt and fear gradually subsides. In its place, over time, a healing tranquility is seeping into my being.

Sayings of the Sages

Then one of the seraphs flew to me, holding in his hand a live coal which he had taken from the altar with a pair of tongs. With this he touched my mouth and said: "See now, this has touched your lips, your sin is taken away, your iniquity is purged."
    —*Isaiah 6:6 & 7*

A Hunk of Healing Humor

Many have quarreled about religion that never practiced it.
    —*Benjamin Franklin*

Daily Affirmation

Today, I experience a healing tranquility.

Twelve Step Thought

Change takes time. How often I've heard those words at meetings! And how frequently I revolted against the tedious truth of that statement! To my poor ego, it seems like I should have reached sainthood by now. Of course, I haven't. However, I have learned some important lessons in recovery. Pray fervently every day to be made whole. Get, and use, a sponsor. Whenever necessary, do another Fourth and Fifth Step. Go to meetings and share there. Do a specific daily Tenth Step in writing. Apologize whenever you're wrong. Pray for those you can't stand. Take time to meditate every day. Finally, keep asking God to remove your defects of character.

Sayings of the Sages

The hour has come for you to wake up from your slumber.
      —*Romans 13:11*

For when a thing is at first very hard to a man and strange, and seemingly quite impossible, if he put all his strength and energy into it, and persevere therein, that will afterward grow quite light and easy, which he at first thought quite out of reach.
      —*Theologia Germanica, VIII*

A Hunk of Healing Humor

Time is a great teacher, but unfortunately it kills all its pupils.
      —*Hector Berlioz*

Daily Affirmation

Change is becoming easier for me.

Twelve Step Thought

Following an unexpected increase in humility, I became quite prepared to let a Higher Power excise all my personality perversions. Somewhere inside me, I intuitively knew that I must relinquish my unhealthy ego. This meant seeking my spiritual guide's direction for me and letting go of *my* preferences. I fearfully imagined the dissolution of my individuality! However, practicing the Twelve Step principles upheld me. The seemingly painful process of transcending self became inevitable and even desirable.

Sayings of the Sages

And in this bringing back and healing, I can, or may, or shall do nothing of myself, but just simply yield to God.
    —*Theologia Germanica, III*

The sage stays behind, thus he is ahead.
    —*Tao Te Ching, 7*

A Hunk of Healing Humor

Don't be humble. You're not that great.
    —*Golda Meir*

Daily Affirmation

I let go, and let God.

Twelve Step Thought

Being "entirely ready" implies an unreserved willingness to keep moving along the path of personal growth. It signifies that one is quite open to the new, the unknown. It means being prepared to risk what is for what can be. In my own case, I felt that I was really risking my familiar self for some scarily transmogrified version of my essence. And, in this present instant, I'm as disposed as I possibly can be for God's healing action to be working in my life. Sometimes, this openness of the seeker is like walking into a holy place permeated with wonders. Drunk with the inhalation of grace, I whisper: "I'm ready, God."

Sayings of the Sages

Who of you by worrying can add a single hour to his life? Since you cannot do this least thing, why do you worry about the rest?
        —*Luke 12:25 & 26*

There are those who cannot free themselves because they are bound by material existence. But nothing can overcome heaven.
        —*Chuang Tsu: Inner Chapters, 6*

A Hunk of Healing Humor

The only man who can change his mind is the man who's got one.
        —*Edward Noyes Westcott*

Daily Affirmation

I'm ready for God's healing action.

Twelve Step Thought

Of course, there are days when I'm a lot less than "entirely ready." These are the occasions when my sick ego wishes to hang on to all its defects. There are times when God is not welcome in my thoughts. There are whole strings of hours when I'm terribly burdened with guilt, fear, shame, and depression. On such negative days, I can hardly get out of bed. Forget about looking forward to some divine tree surgeon sawing off a number of my crooked limbs or character flaws! Just breathing is a major effort. In those moments, I ask my Higher Power to help me break through my resistance. Also, I increase my prayer and meditation.

Sayings of the Sages

Why so downcast, my soul, why do you sigh within me? Put your hope in God: I shall praise him yet, my saviour, my God.
　　—*Psalm 43:5*

The man who . . . remains the same in pain and pleasure, who is wise makes himself fit for eternal life.
　　—*Bhagavad Gita II, 15*

A Hunk of Healing Humor

The god most people believe in couldn't get into heaven.
　　—*William Roylance*

Daily Affirmation

My Higher Power is helping me overcome resistance.

Twelve Step Thought

Practicing Step Six means being focused on the solution rather than being fixated on the problem. Otherwise, it's entirely possible for me to feel crushed beneath the weight of my character defects. Even after sharing the list of my faults with another human being, I can get stuck in reviewing the awful complexity of my mistakes. When I'm busy thinking about the extent of my difficulties, certainly I'm not thinking about God. Actually, when I'm lost in such negative daydreams, I'm refusing to let go and to let God handle it. Being part of the solution involves making myself ready to have God resolve all my weaknesses.

Sayings of the Sages

All that we are arises with our thoughts. With our thoughts we make the world.
    —*Dhammapada, 1*

I am the way and the truth and the life; no one comes to the Father except through me.
    —*John 4:6*

A Hunk of Healing Humor

You can't depend on your eyes when your imagination is out of focus.
    —*Mark Twain*

Daily Affirmation

Today, I'm part of the solution.

Twelve Step Thought

Readying myself to get focused on God, the solution, required some heavy-duty footwork. It took letting go of a bunch of addictive activities as well as pursuing inspirational reading, meditation, honesty, and support group attendance. Before making such efforts in recovery, I struggled uselessly with my obsessive personality through one sick cycle after another. My life was truly unprepared; and it showed. I spent much time wallowing in guilt and in the ever-unfolding shock of long-repressed feelings. Even after quitting the active cycles of addiction, I still was not "ready" for some years. Then, blessed by a spiritual teacher, grace gave me ways of placing myself at a Higher Power's disposal.

Sayings of the Sages

Our hope for you is firm, because we know that just as you share in our sufferings, so also you share in our comfort.
—*II Corinthians 1:7*

In the pursuit of learning, every day something is acquired. In the pursuit of Tao, every day something is dropped.
—*Tao Te Ching, 48*

A Hunk of Healing Humor

The world is filled with willing people; some willing to work, the rest willing to let them.
—*Robert Frost*

Daily Affirmation

I'm placing myself at my Higher Power's disposal.

Twelve Step Thought

When it comes to making tough decisions, it takes me a while to figure things out. For example, it took me years to understand that becoming ready to have God *remove* my defects of character meant preparing for a sort of divine *surgery*. A lively dialogue with myself ensued. I wasn't so crazy about real blood and physical pain, let alone the psychic kinds. Hadn't I suffered enough? "Would you rather go back where you came from?" came the reply. No way! I consented to the dreaded operation, so that my recovery could be complete. Today, I understand that it's always better to trust the divine doctor than the monster of obsession.

Sayings of the Sages

People who "cannot make decisions" are in that state because they have made a decision not to make decisions. They are indecisive because they have been too decisive in the first place. The consequence of precipitate decisiveness must be inactivated if the condition of uncertainty is to be overcome.
    —*Idries Shah, Reflections*

A Hunk of Healing Humor

The only way to keep your health is to eat what you don't want, drink what you don't like, and do what you'd rather not.
    —*Mark Twain*

Daily Affirmation

Today, I trust the divine doctor.

Twelve Step Thought

Now that I have experienced a loving unity with fellow sufferers, I perceive whatever separates me from the true oneness as *the* obstacle to be removed. And I lay my plans at the feet of my Higher Power. Too many times have I realized that my greedy negative ego and my obstinate will were powerless. From a more humbled posture, I can ask for immersion in unifying love instead of fear-filling otherness. I know that I can depend on loving Strength, more powerful than a million suns combined.

Sayings of the Sages

I am the gate; whoever enters through me will be saved.
    —*John 10:9*

Do not think that you know. Be aware of all that is and dwell in the infinite.
    —*Chuang Tsu: Inner Chapters, 7*

A Hunk of Healing Humor

Necessary evil: A character defect we like so much we refuse to do away with it.
    —*Anonymous*

Daily Affirmation

I depend on a loving Strength.

Twelve Step Thought

As I grew in recovery, I gradually developed the trust necessary for placing myself at God's disposal. I came to believe that, somehow, a Higher Power was transforming my flaws into virtues. At first, my tunnel-vision morality made me resist evil. Finally, gaining some spiritual balance, I learned that one of the great mental principles is the Law of Substitution. Whoever attacks an obsessive monster will be overcome. Opposing a negative thought only strengthens it. But when one focuses solely on the radiant virgin, the dragon is slain. The trick is to switch my attention to a positive thought which I find very attractive. In this way, I best prepare myself for the redeeming action of divine energy.

Sayings of the Sages

You should not resist evil.
    —*Matthew 5:39*

In all things whatsoever, seek and intend the glory and praise of God alone. We must not seek our own, either in things spiritual or in things natural. It must needs be thus, if it is to stand well with us.
    —*Theologia Germanica, LIV*

A Hunk of Healing Humor

To put one's trust in God is only a longer way of saying that one will chance it.
    —*Samuel Butler*

Daily Affirmation

Today, I'm focusing on positive thoughts.

Twelve Step Thought

There is a definite relationship between the Sixth Step and that principle wherein I decided to give over my will and my life to the care of my own special Providence. If I seek only the glory and praise of that very Power which is saving my life, then I'll be in sync with the purpose of Step Six. Truly practicing this principle will make the difference between striving for a self-determined objective and for the perfect objective which is of God. Once again, I return to the humble admission of my dependence on a Higher Power. This is that same truth found throughout the annals of philosophy: freedom is found in divine handcuffs.

Sayings of the Sages

Those who with faith, holding Me as their supreme aim, follow this immortal wisdom, those devotees are exceedingly dear to Me.
   —*Bhagavad Gita XII, 20*

There is no worse enemy of the soul than you yourself, if you are not in harmony with the spirit.
   —*The Imitation of Christ III, 13*

A Hunk of Healing Humor

Some people handle the truth carelessly; others never touch it at all.
   —*Anonymous*

Daily Affirmation

I depend on my Higher Power.

Twelve Step Thought

Before becoming ready to have God remove my defects of character, I had to discover what these defective traits were. So I made an inventory and I discussed the contents with a trusted confidant. The list covered a lot of territory. It pointed out my basic problems with self-honesty and with communicativeness. It identified my low self-esteem as well as my inability to express feelings. Since that time, other issues have come to my attention—such as my frequent defensiveness. So I keep track of my needy areas by doing a daily mini-inventory of my liabilities and my assets. Whenever indicated, I take appropriate action to address my mistakes. The outcome is up to God.

Sayings of the Sages

Now that you have been set free from sin and have become slaves to God, the benefit you reap leads to holiness, and the result is eternal life.
    —*Romans 6:22*

I rescue all who cling to me, I protect whoever knows my name.
    —*Psalm 91:14*

A Hunk of Healing Humor

The average man does not know what to do with this life, yet wants another one which will last forever.
    —*Anatole France*

Daily Affirmation

Today, I'm clinging to the divine rescuer.

Twelve Step Thought

The single pressing aspect about Step Six is the soulful need to make a willing and honest start. With obsessions, any major delay in a recuperative course could be deadly. In fact, until I actually began practicing this principle, I found myself being sucked into a black hole of depression and defeatism. First, I was beaten into surrender. Then, I was rescued by a Force beyond myself. I listed and admitted my problems to another. Suddenly, the absolute enormity of the changes required struck me like a bolt of lightning! For some time, I was paralyzed with fear. Then, I renewed my confidence in a Higher Power and a comforting slogan: one day at a time.

Sayings of the Sages

If anyone says to this mountain, "Go, throw yourself into the sea," and . . . believes that what he says will happen, it will be done for him.
    —*Mark 2:23*

Free yourself from pleasure and pain. For, in craving pleasure or in nursing pain, there is only sorrow.
    —*Dhammapada, 16*

A Hunk of Healing Humor

Every one is as God made him and oftentimes a good deal worse.
    —*Cervantes*

Daily Affirmation

One day at a time.

Twelve Step Thought

I see now a paradoxical truth in the ancient adage: "God helps those who help themselves." The Sixth Step is about letting God a little further into my life—thereby consciously benefitting by Providence's greater presence. I must collaborate in increasing my willingness. And I do this by repeating Step Three to the best of my ability. I shy away from my former sick habit of self-sufficiency. Also, I review and accept the fact that it takes sustained personal exertion for me to conform to God's will. Then, I remind myself that my growing freedom is based on turning my will and my life over to the care of my trustworthy Higher Power, Supreme Spiritfire as I understand it.

Sayings of the Sages

The sage works without recognition. He achieves what has to be done without dwelling on it.
    —*Tao Te Ching, 77*

This state of things is all of God's own making. He holds in his power the soul of every living thing, and the breath of each man's body.
    —*Job 12:9 & 10*

A Hunk of Healing Humor

The moment you're born you're done for.
    —*Arnold Bennett*

Daily Affirmation

God helps me when I help myself.

Twelve Step Thought

I've been getting ready for deep changes in my life. Yet, first, I had to learn tremendous trust in a Supreme Principle as I best understood it. My degree of readiness was very much defined by my degree of trust. What a strange dichotomy! Most basically, what I really know is pleasure and pain. In them, I find nothing but disappointment. In the Divine Essence, of which I'm most ignorant, I somehow find meaningfulness and peace of soul. What is this longing for some quite intangible spirit-quality? Even more, I now seek to have a celestial surgeon cut out the cancerous aspects of my character. For this I'm being readied.

Sayings of the Sages

Those who fear him need only to ask to be answered; he hears their cries for help and saves them.
    —*Psalm 145:19*

When really turning toward truth, you will find truth turning toward you.
    —*Vernon Howard*

A Hunk of Healing Humor

To be absolutely certain about something, one must know everything or nothing about it.
    —*Olin Miller*

Daily Affirmation

I find meaning and peace in the Divine.

Twelve Step Thought

I don't think I'm readying myself for the Universal Force to totally eliminate all my natural desires. I'll still get thirsty. I'll still experience hunger pangs. I'll still try to stave off death. I'll still sleep when tired. I'll still seek the company of fellow human beings. I'll still feel the fire of sexual energy in my brain and in my loins. It is the inappropriate manifestations of these "passions" that a Higher Power can remove from me. As long as I'm not hurting anyone else or my inner guide in expressing such drives, what's appropriate is what fits me. What I can't do is define my conduct by someone else's ethics.

Sayings of the Sages

When wisdom comes into your heart and knowledge is a delight to you, then prudence will be there to watch over you, and discernment be your guardian.
        —*Proverbs 2:10 & 11*

Whoever can know life, death, being and non-being all as one, shall be our friend.
        —*Chuang Tsu: Inner Chapters, 6*

A Hunk of Healing Humor

Good breeding consists of concealing how much we think of ourselves and how little we think of other persons.
        —*Mark Twain*

Daily Affirmation

Wisdom is in my heart today.

Twelve Step Thought

Some physicist once quipped that "nature abhors a vacuum." I believe this referred to the fact that there are no perfect vacuums existing naturally in this universe. Similarly, suicide constitutes a vacuum, a human space unnaturally emptied of life. In fact, the desire to end life is a major character fault of our time. Perhaps it's an effort to become one with perceived existential emptiness? How sad! Fortunately, the unconscious often successfully militates against such a desperate act. Both nature and God abhor suicide. Being alive is most necessary to the likely prospect of spiritual growth.

Sayings of the Sages

There is nothing so much in hell as of self-will. . . . When we say self-will, we mean, to will otherwise than as the One and Eternal Will of God willeth.

   —*Theologia Germanica, XLIX*

I am the Living One; I was dead, and behold I am alive for ever and ever! And I hold the keys of death and Hades.

   —*Revelation 1:18*

A Hunk of Healing Humor

The reports of my death are greatly exaggerated.
   —*Mark Twain*

Daily Affirmation

I am alive and growing.

Twelve Step Thought

The truth is that I've been wrestling a long time with my worst character defects. Sure, I'd be overjoyed to have them totally removed from me! Yet, what I get is progress, not perfection. Such improvement is like riding an escalator that spirals upward. As I reach each new level, it seems I must contend with the very same faults again—except with a higher degree of awareness and meaningfulness at each stop. Much as I wish or try to avoid the inevitable, I still carry my past with me. The real question is this: how do I balance this load with the burden I willingly seek to embrace?

Sayings of the Sages

We must suffer these things to be what they are, and enter into the union with God.
—*Theologia Germanica, XXVII*

For him, without concentration, there is no peace; and, for the unpeaceful, how can there be happiness?
—*Bhagavad Gita II, 66*

A Hunk of Healing Humor

People who have no faults are terrible; there is no way of taking advantage of them.
—*Anatole France*

Daily Affirmation

I'm often aware of my progress today.

Twelve Step Thought

Personal growth has proven to be an evolutionary process for me. There have been no visibly instantaneous transformations along my path. Quite oppositely, I've felt the painful cutting edge of failure on many an occasion. I frequently was tempted to stop practicing these principles leading to self-transcendence. Somehow, even if at a sickly snail's pace, I kept moving forward. Little by little, I learned necessary lessons from my repeated errors. And, ever so slowly, my behavior began to reflect a real grasp of my particular learnings. So what if I hadn't met with immediate success in my attempts to change? I was on the way to realization.

Sayings of the Sages

You were once darkness, but now you are light in the Lord. Live as children of light.
　　—Ephesians 5:8

The wise man, following the way, crosses over. . . . He leaves the dark way for the way of light.
　　—Dhammapada, 6

A Hunk of Healing Humor

When you get there, there isn't any there there.
　　—Gertrude Stein

Daily Affirmation

Today, I'm living in the light.

Twelve Step Thought

As I moved along the way of transformation, I gathered more and more self-esteem. I found that I'm really okay—despite all the garbage I have accumulated. Mostly, it was the old puritanical traditions which fostered my being down on myself. After years of beating myself, I was led to discover that I'm basically a good person. My problems only stemmed from some of the methods I was employing for living my life. The tools were defective, not the individual wielding them. With some enlightened assistance, I found that my behaviors could be changed. So my evolution gathered momentum. Now, I even love me.

Sayings of the Sages

Come, let us go up to the mountain of the Lord, to the Temple of the God of Jacob so that he may teach us his ways and we may walk in his paths.
    —*Micah 4:2*

It is more important to see the simplicity, to realize one's true nature, to cast off selfishness and temper desire.
    —*Tao Te Ching, 19*

A Hunk of Healing Humor

It is better to deserve honors and not have them than to have them and not deserve them.
    —*Mark Twain*

Daily Affirmation

I'm really okay.

Twelve Step Thought

Becoming ready for the deletion of my defects turned into a whole personal-development project in itself. I began to sense a latent power in prayer and in meditation for realizing this endeavor. I found that, as I increasingly pursued conscious contact with my Higher Power, my obsessive fear and weakness were being transformed into spiritual strength and understanding. Eventually, it occurred to me that a strong relationship existed between Step Eleven and Step Six. As I grew more tuned in to the Cosmic Vibration and could manage more willingness for doing the divine will, I experienced a geometrically expanding empowerment to start readying myself for grace's corrective action in my soul.

Sayings of the Sages

There are, literally, thousands of wise people, unknown to the ordinary man. They teach in a manner which is not recognized as teaching by the herd. They continuously influence man.
—*Idries Shah, Reflections*

Make a straight highway for our God across the desert.
—*Isaiah 40:3*

A Hunk of Healing Humor

If you can't get a compliment any other way, pay yourself one.
—*Mark Twain*

Daily Affirmation

Today, I'm tuned in to the Cosmic Vibration.

Twelve Step Thought

There are some glaring faults that I'm anxious to have a Higher Power remove. One is my defensiveness. Somewhere along the way, the basement of my being became flooded with paranoia. So, often, it seems someone or something is "trying to do me in." What an ego trip! Could *I* truly be *that* important to others? I doubt it. They're probably too busy worrying about their own mistakes. I'm certain that this psychic stance stems from a sense of inadequacy acquired in childhood. Yet, the reality now is that my life is negatively affected by this self-defensive posture. As for a resolution, I look foward to some divine intervention.

Sayings of the Sages

If you are open to everything you see and hear, and allow this to act through you, even gods and spirits will come to you, not to speak of men.
—*Chuang Tsu: Inner Chapters, 4*

The rising sun will come to us from heaven to shine on those living in darkness ... to guide our feet into the path of peace.
—*Luke 1:78 & 79*

A Hunk of Healing Humor

Politics has become so expensive that it takes a lot of money even to be defeated.
—*Will Rogers*

Daily Affirmation

Guide my feet into the path of peace.

Twelve Step Thought

The bastard child of Aries is the next major fault I would love to see go. I'm referring to anger, a killer who relentlessly stalks me wherever I go. Often, this mad hunter hides in ambush at an unconscious level where I cannot see him. Over the years, I've come to believe that one cause of this defect is the friction and heat generated each time I resist the flow of life. It appears that I frequently fuel the flames of that very fire that I so much fear. Trying to halt the flow or stop the wheel of karma only results in a greater conflagration. I'm entirely ready to be saved from this murderer of peace in my soul.

Sayings of the Sages

Your enemy the devil prowls around like a roaring lion looking about, seeking whom he may devour.
    —*I Peter 5:8*

The Devil and Nature are one, and where nature is conquered the Devil is also conquered.
    —*Theologia Germanica, XLIII*

A Hunk of Healing Humor

Man is a rational animal who always loses his temper when called upon to act in accordance with the dictates of reason.
    —*Oscar Wilde*

Daily Affirmation

Today, I'm flowing with life's currents.

Twelve Step Thought

For me, the trickiest weakness of them all is the withholding of forgiveness. Strangely enough, it has become relatively easy for me to forgive my enemies. It's forgiving close friends who seemingly oppose me that gives me the greatest difficulty and requires the longest time. Perhaps it's that very closeness which makes extending forgiveness so hard. But can anyone truly love another unconditionally without forgiving her or him? I wonder. In any case, for me, truly not forgiving—others or myself—is a costly mistake which fills me with pain. This crazy path of spiritual growth sure isn't easy!

Sayings of the Sages

He whose mind is untroubled in the midst of sorrows and is free from eager desire amid pleasures, he from whom passion, fear, and rage have passed away, he is called a sage of settled intelligence.
    —*Bhagavad Gita II, 56*

Anyone who hospitably receives whomever I may send hospitably receives me.
    —*John 13:20*

A Hunk of Healing Humor

The secret of forgiving everything is to understand nothing.
    —*George Bernard Shaw*

Daily Affirmation

Today, I forgive my friends and myself.

Twelve Step Thought

I need to follow the forceful intuition that wells up confidently from deep within myself. When I don't respond readily, I pay a psychic price. I become obsessed with mundane desires, which then distract me from any promptings of grace. And I don't like this state of distraction. So I try to pay attention—even though this manifestation of mental energy is clearly nonrational. My unhealthy ego attempts to run away from such uncontrollable sureness. It feels threatened by these strong inspirations. Yet, whenever my small self seeks to flee, I find myself turning a deaf ear to the sacred strains of the Wind that blows free. May a Higher Power save me from spiritual deafness.

Sayings of the Sages

The Tao of heaven does not strive, and yet it overcomes. It does not speak, and yet it is answered. It does not ask, yet is supplied with all its needs.
> —*Tao Te Ching, 73*

You will receive power when the Holy Spirit comes on you.
> —*Acts 1:8*

A Hunk of Healing Humor

I don't know of a single foreign product that enters this country untaxed, except the answer to prayer.
> —*Mark Twain*

Daily Affirmation

I'm following the intuition from deep within.

Twelve Step Thought

At times, the lethargy of plain laziness muffles some marvelous melodies. When that happens, I'm settling for only as much perfection as will get me by in life. Then, I usually discover that I'm really in a "downer" mode. Other times, I find that my body and my emotions are crying out for an "upper"—and almost any stimulant will do. On such occasions, I'm tempted to lose myself totally in the excitement of gambling or "pigging out" or having sex fantasies or shopping way beyond my limit. Boy, am I ever obsessive! Yet, I want so much to grow. So I'll listen more intently for the voice from within.

Sayings of the Sages

Whether you turn to right or left, your ears will hear these words behind you, "This is the way, follow it."
—*Isaiah 30:21 & 22*

Why do what you will regret? Why bring tears upon yourself? Do only what you do not regret, and fill yourself with joy.
—*Dhammapada, 5*

A Hunk of Healing Humor

It should be easy to make an honest living—there's so little competition.
—*Herbert Prochnow*

Daily Affirmation

Today, I'm listening for divine melodies.

Twelve Step Thought

I oppose readiness to a degree by holding on to some junk that I'm not yet prepared to give up. In a way, I prefer throwing manure at the flies. Why let go of cherished resentments? Because, deep down, letting go means forgetting my preferences and remembering the Universe's wishes. Herein, my greatest strength becomes my greatest obstacle. My tenacious will to grow turns into stubborn resistance to those very changes which would spur the most growth. What a supremely difficult and strangely paradoxical task! First, I'm ready. Then, I'm not ready. That very mind which avidly seeks liberation sorely restrains me at times. So I cry out for help from my Higher Power deep within.

Sayings of the Sages

So Man, when he resteth and assureth himself upon divine Protection and Favor, gathereth a Force and Faith which Human Nature, in itself, could not obtain.
  —*Francis Bacon*

Where there is pride, and a haughty spirit, and a light careless mind, Christ is not, nor any true follower of his.
  —*Theologia Germanica, XXVI*

A Hunk of Healing Humor

Few minds wear out; more rust out.
  —*Christian Nestell Bovee*

Daily Affirmation

I'm counting on divine protection and favor.

Twelve Step Thought

Sincerely becoming ready meant first believing that a Higher Power *could* remove my defects of character. Why not? Hadn't I already seen my overwhelming obsession taken away? Working Steps Two and Three had set the stage for acquiring this additional conviction. Even more, in completing my Fifth Step, I experienced forgiveness—blame and guilt being lifted—both as a receiver and as a giver. Once again, I'm recognizing the need for powerful assistance in making even more progress. For my part, I'm willing to do the footwork directed toward a richer recovery. I have much motivation for being further transformed. And my openness to divine intervention is increasing.

Sayings of the Sages

Heaven's net casts wide. Though its meshes are course, nothing slips through.
—*Tao Te Ching, 73*

To those who believed in his name, he gave the right to become children of God.
—*John 1:12*

A Hunk of Healing Humor

Martyrdom has always been a proof of the intensity, never of the correctness of a belief.
—*Arthur Schnitzler*

Daily Affirmation

I'm receiving powerful assistance in making more progress.

Twelve Step Thought

In my mind, the words *entirely ready* mean that I'm reaching for the highest ideal imaginable. Along with this aspiration, I'm more open to the spirit welling up within me. I really seek the best or the ultimate good. For me, such a *good* is divinity spelled with four letters. Step Six is a method of demonstrating an appropriate attitude toward my search. In seeking readiness, I'm barely beginning a course of spiritual growth. Yet, when all else has turned negative for me, now I'm willing to trust my Higher Power to get me through the night. And I hold in my heart a strong expectation that some saving grace will carry me across the wasteland which surrounds me.

Sayings of the Sages

Be content with the moment, and be willing to follow the flow; then there will be no room for grief or joy. In the old days this was called freedom from bondage.
    —*Chuang Tsu: Inner Chapters, 3*

Have nothing to do with godless myths and old wives' tales; rather, train yourself to be godly.
    —*I Timothy 4:7*

A Hunk of Healing Humor

People who stay in the middle of the road get run over.
    —*Aneurin Bevan*

Daily Affirmation

Saving grace is carrying me across.

Twelve Step Thought

To the best of my ability, I'm slowly making progress in the building of character. Fortunately, a growing internal strength is helping to propel me forward. I'm becoming ready to have my Higher Power remove more obsession and mania from my life. In so doing, I exert great mental cooperation with the purifying divine action. Whoever said the footwork was easy? Closely examined, a program of personal development is fairly complex. And it requires a whole lot of hard effort! I'm forced to continually refocus my mind. In order to collaborate more completely with my purification, I must repeatedly tune in to the vibration of spirit.

Sayings of the Sages

Don't be afraid; just believe.
> —*Mark 5:36*

Among thousands of persons scarcely one strives for perfection; and, of those who strive and succeed, scarcely one knows Me in truth.
> —*Bhagavad Gita VII, 3*

A Hunk of Healing Humor

I am far too righteous to ever be sanctimonious.
> —*William Roylance*

Daily Affirmation

I'm tuning in to the vibration of spirit.

Twelve Step Thought

Some say that only Step One can be practiced with absolute perfection. Then, the other eleven steps could be thought of as perfect ideals—never totally attainable. In that sense, I'm becoming really ready to walk in the direction of perfection. Once again, the major emphasis is on "willingness." Such a comprehensive word! At times, it includes much more than I wish to face. Yet, to keep on keeping on, I must be willing to do whatever is necessary. Additionally, I like to believe that the steps *could* be lived to perfection. In reality, "perfection" means completeness or wholeness of being. And I'm ready to become whole—filling the addictive hole in the middle of me.

Sayings of the Sages

Know the truth and find peace.
   —*Dhammapada, 1*

Achieve results, but never glory in them. Achieve results, but never boast. Achieve results, but never be proud. Achieve results, because this is the natural way.
   —*Tao Te Ching, 30*

A Hunk of Healing Humor

Our eyes are placed in front because it is more important to look ahead than look back.
   —*Herbert Prochnow*

Daily Affirmation

I'm walking toward perfection.

Twelve Step Thought

Without Steps Six and Seven, our rehabilitation to wholeness wouldn't be possible. This is because recovery means becoming open to receiving help—thereby truly accepting that I'm powerless over my addiction. Ah, what a threat to my immature ego! Even more, I should *humbly* ask my Higher Power to remove all my short-comings? This surely is ego deflation! It's funny how assistance from another is essential for restoring peace in the depths of *my* being. My "normal" mode is feeling threatened by the possible intrusion of others. Yet, with a willing mind and heart, I can receive even the searing succor of Spiritfire.

Sayings of the Sages

For him who has conquered his lower self by the Higher Self, his Self is a friend; but for him who has not possessed his higher Self, his very Self will act . . . like an enemy.
    —*Bhagavad Gita VI, 6*

My ways are not your ways.
    —*Isaiah 55:8*

A Hunk of Healing Humor

I can believe anything providing it is incredible.
    —*Oscar Wilde*

Daily Affirmation

My higher Self is my friend.

Twelve Step Thought

I no longer savor the shallowness of my separate existence. In trying to transcend negative ego, my shadow self, I sought the help of a more comprehensive consciousness. For me, negative ego is the insistence on *my* separateness. And my shadow self lurks ominously as the unseen pattern of my unwanted personality traits. Yet, my needs are always met—as long as I perform the footwork. Insights arrive. I am experiencing gradual, one-step-at-a-time transformation. The benefits of such seeking are now obvious.

Sayings of the Sages

For if mine eye is to see anything, it must be single, or else be purified from all other things.
> —*Theologia Germanica, I*

Being perfectly harmonized, he resorts to Me alone as the highest goal.
> —*Bhagavad Gita VII, 18*

A Hunk of Healing Humor

Some geniuses are conceited; but I'm not.
> —*Anonymous*

Daily Affirmation

My Higher Power is removing my shortcomings.

Twelve Step Thought

There was a time when I tried to live solely by my own strength. I paid only lip service to a vague source of supernatural energy. That approach to living caused me a lot of suffering. A solution dawned for me when I selected a much more appropriate target for my confidence. On this topic, I recall some striking words of Teresa of Avila: "All our efforts are unavailing unless we completely give up having confidence in ourselves and fix it all upon God." I found that this kind of effort requires a fair degree of humility. Today, I can more and more often *humbly* request that my shortcomings be removed.

Sayings of the Sages

Beware of the teachers of the law. They like to walk around in flowing robes and love to be greeted in the marketplaces and have the . . . places of honor at banquets.
    —*Luke 20:46*

Far inferior indeed is mere action to the discipline of intelligence . . . seek refuge in intelligence.
    —*Bhagavad Gita II, 49*

A Hunk of Healing Humor

It is easy for a somebody to be modest, but it is difficult to be modest when one is a nobody.
    —*Jules Renard*

Daily Affirmation

I place all confidence in my Higher Power

Twelve Step Thought

I came to rely on a Higher Power to transform the unhealthy state of my inner self. For a long time, the ego aspect of my mind served mostly as a negativity generator—projecting a very fearful reality upon the screen of my consciousness. In reaction, I hid behind a wall of compulsion and addiction. There is a lot less "head-tripping" in the thrust of growth that I am experiencing. Sometimes, when faced with anger or seeming attack from another, I can actually radiate peace by trusting my Higher Power and by reacting with unconditional love.

Sayings of the Sages

I answer everyone who invokes me, I am with them when they are in trouble.
—*Psalm 91:15*

Why does everyone like the Tao so much at first? Isn't it because you find what you seek . . . ?
—*Tao Te Ching, 62*

A Hunk of Healing Humor

Everybody is ignorant, only on different subjects.
—*Will Rogers*

Daily Affirmation

My Higher Power radiates unconditional love.

Twelve Step Thought

The sages say that humility is truth. And, when I'm being humble or truthful, I'm being honest about the reality of my situation. Yet, when I reach out honestly, I expose the frail bosom of my being. How can I avoid being hurt when I so open myself? The answer is devastatingly simple: *I can't*. I could really worry about this. Then again, I could trust the Source of this universal flow. Each day, each moment: the choice is up to me. In Michelangelo's magnificent Sistine Chapel fresco, God reaches out to touch man. When I opt for real growth, I reach out to touch God.

Sayings of the Sages

The greatest Virtue is to follow Tao and Tao alone. The Tao is elusive and intangible. . . . Oh, it is dim and dark, and yet within is essence. This essence is very real, and therein lies faith.
—*Tao Te Ching, 21*

Did you receive the Holy Spirit when you believed?
—*Acts 19:2*

A Hunk of Healing Humor

Everyone wishes to have truth on his side, but not everyone wishes to be on the side of truth.
—*Richard Whately*

Daily Affirmation

I'm touching God today.

Twelve Step Thought

Some wise persons once said that there are three main roads to hell: inordinate desire, anger, and greed. I wish to avoid all of them. In this sense, when a shortcoming is being removed from me, my Higher Power is guiding me away from the pathways to Hades. Of course, some willing effort is necessary on my part. I must actively avoid selfish wishes. I must redirect hateful energy when it arises. I must back off *attachment* to material possessions. In so doing, I rely on a loving Force much greater than my own. And, faced with such saving Strength and with the richness of God's children, I can be humble.

Sayings of the Sages

All things occurred through him, and not one thing occurred without him.
>   —*John 1:3*

It is hard to live in the world and hard to live out of it.
>   —*Dhammapada, 21*

A Hunk of Healing Humor

A great many open minds should be closed for repairs.
>   —*Toledo Blade*

Daily Affirmation

I'm cooperating with my loving Guide.

Twelve Step Thought

In seeking greater growth, I'm beginning to recognize the *absolute necessity* of relying on a greater-than-myself Power. Prior experience indicates I can't accomplish anything alone. Surely recovering and expanding are no exceptions! Even my confidence in a friendly Force is a gift from God. Being able to philosophically prove Divinity's existence isn't the source of a working faith. Neither are apparent triumphs over life's trials. Rather, when I open myself to direction, when I gently humble myself, when I wait for the unannounced moment of grace, then I'm filled with believing and I'm propelled forward.

Sayings of the Sages

The sage dwells among those things which can never be lost, and so he lives forever.
　　—*Chuang Tsu: Inner Chapters, 6*

There is none apart from me. Turn to me and be saved, all the ends of the earth, for I am God unrivalled.
　　—*Isaiah 45:21 & 22*

A Hunk of Healing Humor

Never believe anything until it has been officially denied.
　　—*Claud Cockburn*

Daily Affirmation

I rely on my Higher Power in all things.

Twelve Step Thought

Asking is essential to the practice of Step Seven. And it's in prayer that I most appropriately ask God for help. Next to meditation, to me prayer represents the highest type of human mental energy. So I humbly focus on praying as a means for obtaining divine assistance to transform my character defects. As well as needing to ask, I also need to go beyond asking. Getting in touch with a Higher Power has many more aspects. For me, prayer is a holistic activity. In it, I thank God for recovery; through it, I contribute to a state of spiritual fitness. I relish the whole spectrum of prayer—from pleading for boons to praising God's glories.

Sayings of the Sages

Pray for each other so that you may be healed. The prayer of a righteous man is powerful and effective.
    —*James 5:16*

Let him therefore who wisheth that God should help him to what is best, and best for him, give diligent heed to God's counsels and teachings. . . . Thus, and not else, will he have . . . God's help.
    —*Theologia Germanica, XXXIV*

A Hunk of Healing Humor

I do count my many blessings, but people call me conceited.
    —*William Roylance*

Daily Affirmation

Today, I'm focused on praying.

Twelve Step Thought

A great paradox is involved in my asking Energy Almighty to remove all my shortcomings. On one hand, the Universe's all-knowing lovingness responds by eliminating obstacles to my growth; on the other hand, Divine Wisdom thereby shatters the illusory power of my isolated perspective and of my addictive delusion that *"now* I've got it all together." It has been stated on occasion that the Divinity tries or chastens those it loves. Kahlil Gibran put it this way in *The Prophet*: "Even as love crowns you so shall he crucify you." Also, "Your pain is the breaking of the shell that encloses your understanding."

Sayings of the Sages

Those whom I love, I rebuke and chasten. Therefore, be zealous and repent.
    —*Revelation 3:19*

It is good for us sometimes to suffer contradiction, to be misjudged by men even though we do well and mean well.
    —*The Imitation of Christ I, 12*

A Hunk of Healing Humor

Happiness is the interval between periods of unhappiness.
    —*Don Marquis*

Daily Affirmation

Pain is the breaking of the shell that encloses my understanding.

Twelve Step Thought

Accepting *how* Cosmic Might removes my shortcomings requires a lot of humility on my part. In fact, such removals have not occurred in any manner that I have anticipated. For one thing, I planned a much less painful approach to the elimination of my character defects. I expected my Higher Power to take away my faults *before* I experienced them anymore. I imagined rapid progress in becoming a better person. I got just the opposite! At times, my recovery was riddled with pain. On the way out, my faults seem intensified and determined to stick to me. And the changing of my behavior is taking a long time. I'm learning to humbly accept God's way.

Sayings of the Sages

Your God was training you as a man trains his child.
  —*Deuteronomy 8:5*

Many people who cannot reach higher think that their arms should be longer. In some cases you can see that it is their legs which are too short.
  —*Idries Shah, Reflections*

A Hunk of Healing Humor

All you need is ignorance and confidence, and then success is sure.
  —*Mark Twain*

Daily Affirmation

Today, I accept God's way.

Twelve Step Thought

Deep in my heartspace, I've felt a searching for the soothing salve of grace. This internal pressure seeks to be expressed, to be verbalized. And this pressing need is in response to my growth being blocked by character defects. On the "outside," this inner momentum is reflected in deciding to call my sponsor and in sharing honestly at closed meetings. For me, what most effectively bridges the gap between "inside" and "outside" are prayer and meditation. Once again, I glimpse the multiple relationships between the Steps as well as how the Steps respond admirably to my needs.

Sayings of the Sages

I am the desire in all beings which is not contrary to their inmost constitution.
    —*Bhagavad Gita VII, 11*

I am convinced that neither death nor life, neither angels nor demons, neither the present nor the future . . . neither height nor depth nor any creature will be able to separate us from the love of God.
    —*Romans 8:38 & 39*

A Hunk of Healing Humor

I wish people who have trouble communicating would just shut up.
    —*Tom Lehrer*

Daily Affirmation

Nothing can separate me from the love of God.

Twelve Step Thought

Oftentimes I found that appropriately dealing with my shortcomings proved painful. I was an eyewitness at the horrible execution of some defects. On occasion, I was numb with fear. Quite clearly, a measure of relief was needed. But to be soothed I had to get humble. Why? Because I had finally discovered that humility is a healer of pain. As I more often humbly accept that I'm powerless over everything, I more readily find strength in the arms of my Higher Power. Then, I feel guided and cared for.

Sayings of the Sages

To act justly, to love tenderly and to walk humbly with your God.
    —*Micah 6:8*

The humble man enjoys peace in the midst of many vexations, because his trust is in God, not in the world.
    —*The Imitation of Christ II, 2*

A Hunk of Healing Humor

So I don't have any humility—that's the only virtue I don't have.
    —*William Roylance*

Daily Affirmation

Humility is a healer of pain.

Twelve Step Thought

Having asked, I receive a response. I find that some Loving Strength is indeed taking away the egotistical obstacle to my shining forth. As limitations are being lifted from me, that which covers the lamp of my spirit is being removed. Thus, ever so gradually, I become a light unto myself and to those around me. As grace shines out from me, I serve as an example to other people. In honestly sharing my experience, strength, and hope with others, a Higher Power beams out a grace-filled radiance. Yet, from a humble perspective, I know the light that shines is not mine.

Sayings of the Sages

You are the light of the world. A city set on a hill cannot be hidden. Nor do people light a lamp and put it under a basket.
        —*Matthew 5:14 & 15*

Day and night, the man who is awake shines in the radiance of the spirit.
        —*Dhammapada, 26*

A Hunk of Healing Humor

It's taken me all my life to understand that it is not necessary to understand everything.
        —*Rene Coty*

Daily Affirmation

Today, my Higher Power beams out light from me.

Twelve Step Thought

Acquiring greater humility is the generative principle for each step in the process of personal development. All the sages teach this truth. When I isolate within the shell of my negative ego, I find that I'm helpless. In order to ascend to a higher level of growth, I need the strength that comes from my Greater Self. Yet, for this saving force to arrive, my attitude and posture must become more humble. Then, when adversity threatens to overwhelm me, I'm more ready for any emergency. It works best when I begin and end each day with a humble prayer.

Sayings of the Sages

The highest good is like water. Water gives life to the ten thousand things and does not strive. It flows in places men reject and so is like the Tao.
    —Tao Te Ching, 8

The Lord will rescue me from every evil attack and will bring me safely to his heavenly kingdom.
    —II Timothy 4:18

A Hunk of Healing Humor

He's so conceited, he has his X-rays retouched.
    —Louis A. Safian

Daily Affirmation

The Lord will rescue me from every evil attack.

Twelve Step Thought

In the context of pursuing continued personal growth, being humble means to quit bluffing and to honestly give God a chance for removing obstacles. This means backing off my old egocentric ways. Deep down inside, I do know that my little ego isn't the center of the universe. Yet, it's imperative that I seek the de facto Center of all that is. In so doing, I'm legitimately expressing a desire to identify and to accomplish God's will. Herein lies the hub of all humility. Such an approach is truly going with the flow of the great universal unfolding. In truth, God acts in its own time and in its own way.

Sayings of the Sages

Selfish intentions divorce from God; and Omnipotence, put to the test, confounds the foolish.
    —*Wisdom 1:3*

Heaven and earth grow together with me, and the ten thousand things and I are one.
    —*Chuang Tsu: Inner Chapters, 2*

A Hunk of Healing Humor

A man learns to skate by staggering about making a fool of himself.
    —*George Bernard Shaw*

Daily Affirmation

I'm giving God a chance to remove my shortcomings.

Twelve Step Thought

In order to prevent a retreat into obsession and active addiction, my character flaws must be dealt with. To this end, practicing Step Seven is a key component of an effective relapse prevention program. It's such preventive medicine that keeps my chronic ailment in remission—similar to keeping cancer or diabetes at bay. Whatever the future may hold, all I have is a daily reprieve based on the fitness of my spiritual condition. As a person who is ongoingly subject to the sickness of addiction, I humbly ask the Divine Doctor to help me become more spiritually fit. Trusting H.P., I focus on living today.

Sayings of the Sages

Be assured that no one can be enlightened unless he be first cleansed or purified and stripped.
　　—Theologia Germanica, XIV

Strive for this, pray for this, desire this—to be stripped of all selfishness.
　　—The Imitation of Christ III, 37

A Hunk of Healing Humor

I shall stay the way I am
Because I do not give a damn.
　　—Dorothy Parker

Daily Affirmation

The Divine Doctor is making me spiritually fit.

Twelve Step Thought

I cannot honestly ask God to remove my shortcomings when I still see satisfying my natural desires as the principal purpose of life. How hypocritical I would be! Who am I really kidding when I act like I live only to make money, have sexual intercourse, eat, wield power, and oppress my fellow humans? Anyway, when I lived for those things, there was never enough of what I thought I wanted. My active addiction sure proved that to me—demanding more . . . more . . . more. . . . Could it be that the old Judeo-Christian legacy is true? If so, the purpose of my life is to know, love, and serve God.

Sayings of the Sages

Rescue begins the moment one discovers that *his* truth is not *the* truth.
    —*Vernon Howard*

When you give a banquet, invite the poor, the crippled, the lame, the blind, and you will be blessed.
    —*Luke 14:13 & 14*

A Hunk of Healing Humor

A thing worth having is a thing worth cheating for.
    —*W. C. Fields*

Daily Affirmation

God is the purpose of my life.

Twelve Step Thought

Again and again, beset by the urges and cravings of my obsessive-compulsive nature, I'm reduced to begging my Higher Power for merciful relief. When I'm stuck in this crazy mode, sometimes I can barely stay away from the addictive solution, let alone ask the Cosmic Force to take away my character defects! Also, when in the grip of desperate thoughts and feelings, I'm really not tuned in to getting humble. To avoid this paradoxical trap, I must return to Step Two—renewing my belief that a Power greater than myself can restore me to sanity. What a tightly woven pattern there is to recovery!

Sayings of the Sages

A man is deficient in understanding until he perceives that there is a whole cycle of evolution possible within himself: repeating endlessly, offering opportunities for personal development.
        —*Idries Shah, Reflections*

Lord, you have been our refuge age after age.
        —*Psalm 90:1*

A Hunk of Healing Humor

Any fool can criticize, and many of them do.
        —*Archbishop C. Garbett*

Daily Affirmation

I'm seeing my opportunities today.

Twelve Step Thought

I have a vision of humility as a major pathway leading to true freedom of spirit. Also, I've learned traveling is easier while leaning on a walking stick. On a spiritual plane, for the time being, I find that I need such support. Otherwise, I fall easily. When my life is directed toward the humble path, it seems like giant steps are being taken toward total liberation. As my ego stays in the background, my Higher Power is effectively in the foreground—carrying me along some miracle way to ever-greater fulfillment. And I trust the Gracegiver that carries me.

Sayings of the Sages

Blessed are the poor in spirit, for theirs is the kingdom of heaven.
 —*Matthew 5:3*

In that purity of spirit, there is produced for him an end of all sorrow.
 —*Bhagavad Gita II, 65*

A Hunk of Healing Humor

There is no unhappiness like the misery of sighting land again after a cheerful, careless voyage.
 —*Mark Twain*

Daily Affirmation

I'm on a path leading to freedom.

Twelve Step Thought

When I implore the Universal Being to transform my
failings, I readily believe that my prayer will be
answered. How can the Source of all creation possibly
be a miser? Even beyond the miracle of human life on
earth, consider the innumerable galaxies that spread
divine splendor infinitely wide. How can there be any
limit to the "isness" of divinity? Thus, God's love has
to be unconditional. Therefore, that Love will always be
there to support me. Such a glorious intuition results in
deep longing for complete conscious contact with my
Lover!

Sayings of the Sages

There is an abstruse astrologer that saith: if it were not
for two things that are constants (. . . that the fixed
stars ever stand at like distance . . . that the diurnal
motion perpetually keepeth time), no individual would
last one moment.
    —*Francis Bacon*

A Hunk of Healing Humor

Love's like the measles, all the worse when it comes
late.
    —*Douglas Jerrold*

Daily Affirmation

God loves me unconditionally.

Twelve Step Thought

For many years, I wanted what I wanted when I wanted it. I was one very self-centered individual. Yet, I was too proud to request what I really *needed* from any man or any god. When I began humbly asking for help, I started to experience a change in attitude that slowly allowed me to move away from me toward God and my fellow seekers. This transformation did not evolve out of my efforts. Rather, it was the grace of God that commenced doing for me what I couldn't do for myself. Gradually, I'm growing less egocentric. My lifework includes responding to the needs of others and to the still, small voice within.

Sayings of the Sages

A man can achieve his own happiness only by pursuing the happiness of others, because it is only by forgetting about his own happiness that he can become happy.
    —D. C. Law

Listen to my cry for help, my King and my God!
    —Psalm 5:2

A Hunk of Healing Humor

While man's desires and aspirations stir he cannot choose but err.
    —Goethe

Daily Affirmation

Today, I'm moving toward God.

Twelve Step Thought

After many years in recovery, I really see the transmission of dysfunctional behavior from one generation to the next. In ancient times, this inheritance of traits was construed as God remembering the iniquities of our forefathers—being punished across generations for disobedience. And in some ways, the "sins" of the parents *are* visited upon the children. Though I tried to be different from my father and mother, somehow I inherited some of the same burdens they had carried. Strewn deep in my unconscious, only later were these seeds to bloom. Clean out my psyche, O Higher Power, and fill me with your fiery spirit.

Sayings of the Sages

Do not hold our ancestors' crimes against us, in tenderness quickly intervene.
　　—Psalm 79:8

God, create a clean heart in me, put into me a new and constant spirit.
　　—Psalm 51:10

A Hunk of Healing Humor

The reason the way of the transgressor is hard is because it's so crowded.
　　—Kin Hubbard

Daily Affirmation

My Higher Power is cleaning out my psyche.

Twelve Step Thought

I can no longer afford to get fixated on my ego's unsatisfied demands. Why? Because I found no peace of mind until I began diminishing my claims for satisfaction. Clamoring for my wants only brought me back to an active state of obsession. Whenever that happened, I felt extremely uncomfortable. Then, I started to act out my discomfort. To avoid any lapse from my recovering status, I must reduce my requiring of whatever. So I humbly ask the Spirit of Love to remove my demandingness. For me, it's a matter of relapse prevention, of life or death. My soul is peaceful to the extent that I let go of egoistic requirements.

Sayings of the Sages

The world and its desires pass away, but the man who does the will of God lives forever.
    —*I John 2:17*

Flow with whatever may happen and let your mind be free.
    —*Chuang Tsu: Inner Chapters, 4*

A Hunk of Healing Humor

Let's have an intelligent conversation. I'll talk and you listen.
    —*William Roylance*

Daily Affirmation

The Spirit of Love is removing my demandingness.

Twelve Step Thought

Today, I'm willing to ask for help in addressing my character defects. For many years, I wouldn't share my problems or seek assistance from anyone. Talk about learning a lesson the hard way! It was only through repeated humiliations that I was prodded into trying humility. Finally, I admitted I was powerless over obsession—this being a most necessary first step toward liberation from its grip. This admission required a healthy minimum degree of getting humble. After that, the big hurdle was actually asking for help. And I found that, even in recovery, I was hurting enough to implore a Higher Power to relieve my obsessiveness.

Sayings of the Sages

Your worst enemy cannot harm you as much as your own thoughts, unguarded.
　　—*Dhammapada, 3*

What god can compare with you: taking fault away?
　　—*Micah 7:18*

A Hunk of Healing Humor

Do not do unto others as you would that they should do unto you. Their tastes may not be the same.
　　—*George Bernard Shaw*

Daily Affirmation

My Higher Power is relieving my obsessiveness.

Twelve Step Thought

Gaining some humility helped relieve my obsessiveness. Gradually, I opened up to learning that becoming increasingly humble could benefit all of my life. So humbleness became a tool that facilitated the removal of other shortcomings. To say the least, I haven't always been thrilled by the puncturing of my negative me-balloon. Yet, I'm now discovering a tremendous personal growth value that is derived from the reduction of my grandiosity and other antagonistic ego traits. Also, rather than listen to my own deprecating self-talk, I'm more willing to hear the still, small voice from deep within.

Sayings of the Sages

How infinitely small is that which makes him a man! How infinitely great is that which makes him perfect in heaven!
    —*Chuang Tsu: Inner Chapters, 5*

Anyone who will not receive the kingdom of God like a little child will never enter it.
    —*Luke 18:17*

A Hunk of Healing Humor

The more you say, the less people remember.
    —*Francois Fenelon*

Daily Affirmation

Today, some humility is benefitting my life.

Twelve Step Thought

My sincere willingness to turn all control over to my Higher Power is essential to my remaining in recovery. My readiness for Divine Strength to take away character defects which impede my serving God and fellow human beings is the main ingredient of my personal growth. When I'm truly ready and I act accordingly, I have completed Step Seven. My humble supplication is, without doubt, an act of faith. Yet, as the ancient adage teaches: faith without works is dead. Thus, now is when my Twelfth Step work really must begin. And humble works involve service for God's glory and the betterment of all women and men.

Sayings of the Sages

My servant will prosper, he shall be lifted up, exalted, rise to great heights.
    —*Isaiah 52:13*

Let every man prove himself, how he standeth towards God.
    —*Theologia Germanica, X*

A Hunk of Healing Humor

I like work; it fascinates me. I can sit and look at it for hours.
    —*Jerome K. Jerome*

Daily Affirmation

I'm giving God credit for whatever I do.

Twelve Step Thought

A strange thing happened one day after I had been recovering for some years. It was like a bright bulb was turned on in the dark depths of my mind. I began to seek out the humble state as something I really *wanted* rather than as something I *must* do. In fact, whatever the nature of the consequences, I found myself constantly looking for truth and humility. It had taken me a long time to arrive at this point. I now see humility as a condition to be desired solely for itself. So I willingly work on garnering all the humility I can. Why? Because, when I'm humble, I feel clean and peaceful.

Sayings of the Sages

The sage is shy and humble—to the world he seems confusing. Men look to him and listen. He behaves like a little child.
    —*Tao Te Ching, 49*

If we claim to be without sin, we deceive ourselves and the truth is not in us.
    —*I John 1:8*

A Hunk of Healing Humor

There's such a thing as moderation, even in telling the truth.
    —*Vera Johnson*

Daily Affirmation

When I'm humble, I'm peaceful.

Twelve Step Thought

I finally realized that humility precludes fear. And the biggest cause of my defects has been self-centered fear. For a long time, I was stuck. I either feared that I would lose some "treasure" I already possessed or that I wouldn't get some "goodie" I had been seeking. Then, I found the Steps. Here was a sure path that, sincerely and thoroughly followed, left no room for fear. So I surrendered all my imperfections to a Higher Power, and asked this Force to lift them from me. Most important, I sought to fully subject my will to God. It just seemed like that effort went along with being humble.

Sayings of the Sages

If the wicked man renounces all the sins he has committed ... and is law-abiding and honest, he will certainly live.
    —*Ezekiel 18:21*

Humility itself does not bring an automatic reward: it is a means to an end.
    —*Idries Shah, Reflections*

A Hunk of Healing Humor

The advantage of the emotions is that they lead us astray.
    —*Oscar Wilde*

Daily Affirmation

Working the Steps is making me fearless.

Twelve Step Thought

In sharp contradiction to this world of *more*, gaining some humility means subscribing to *less*. What a revelation this was to me! I find this recovery business is riddled with similar paradoxes. Ideally, the humble is the true. The truth is that I'm much happier when I seek my Inner Guide's direction rather than following the impulses for *more* from my little ego's greediness. When I slow my thought process, my mind works better. In fact, when I do less than my grandiosity prompts for, my actual accomplishments are always greater. As my attitude grows increasingly humble, my inner peace increases—all per my Guide's words: if things come, let them come; if they go, let them go.

Sayings of the Sages

Treating alike pleasure and pain, gain and loss, victory and defeat, get ready for battle, lest you fall into evil.
—*Bhagavad Gita II, 38*

Do everything in moderation.
—*Anonymous*

A Hunk of Healing Humor

To me, old age is always ten years older than I am.
—*Bernard Baruch*

Daily Affirmation

Today, I'm becoming more peaceful.

Twelve Step Thought

Humility is ever more becoming an ingredient which nourishes my serenity. I have found that a humble attitude can transform even failure and misery into valuable assets. That sounds like a preposterous claim, doesn't it? Yet, in my own life, the veracity of that statement has been demonstrated time and time again. Seemingly terrible situations—like losing a certain job or tearfully crawling across the carpet by my finger-nails—were some of the most helpful events in my life. As more shortcomings are removed, I'm reminded that my humble prayers are being answered. Consequently, I feel more serene.

Sayings of the Sages

Whoever lives by the truth comes into the light, so that it may be seen plainly that his deeds have been done through God.
　　　—John 3:21

The greater you are, the more you should behave humbly, and then you will find favour with the Lord.
　　　—Ecclesiasticus 3:20

A Hunk of Healing Humor

To avoid that run-down feeling, cross streets carefully.
　　　—Jacob Braude

Daily Affirmation

A humble attitude is transforming my life.

Twelve Step Thought

When I truly get humble, I reconcile myself to the Universe's way of unfolding. Really acquiring humility hinges on my willingness to develop and carry out a plan for suppressing self-centeredness. And, graced by my Higher Power, I'm taking the planned steps for reducing my negative ego. I want to follow the Divine Flow. Yet, how will I definitely know God's will for me? What a question! I pondered it for a long time. Out of the blue one day, my best friend gave me the answer: whatever happens to me *is* God's will. The truth is so simple! So now I'm focused on becoming humbler and simpler.

Sayings of the Sages

Temptation cannot touch the man who is awake, strong and humble, who masters himself and minds the law.
—*Dhammapada, 1*

Joy and gladness for all who seek you! To all who love your saving power give constant cause to say, "God is Great!"
—*Psalm 40:16*

A Hunk of Healing Humor

We can't all be heroes because somebody has to sit on the curb and clap as they go by.
—*Will Rogers*

Daily Affirmation

Whatever happens to me is God's will.

Twelve Step Thought

Having my shortcomings removed means being restored to health. For example, once an infected tooth is extracted, the mouth becomes healthy again. Healthiness implies a state of balance, wherein all the parts remain in proportion to one another. Thus, the removal of my defects happens in direct proportion with my willingness to work for recovery. Not only must I declare that I am willing, but I must also do the footwork that is necessary for fully expressing willingness. Finally, I must use all the human resources at my disposal. This being done, I turn all outcomes over to my Higher Power.

Sayings of the Sages

Whoever is thirsty, let him come; and whoever wishes, let him take the free gift of the water of life.
—*Revelation 22:17*

The sage harmonizes right with wrong and rests in the balance of nature.
—*Chuang Tsu: Inner Chapters, 2*

A Hunk of Healing Humor

I have never liked working. To me a job is an invasion of privacy.
—*Danny McGoorty*

Daily Affirmation

I'm being restored to health.

Twelve Step Thought

When I perceive that I have hurt myself or others, I can own my action and be willing to rectify the situation. It took me a while to learn this essential lesson in personal/spiritual growth. In fact, the stability of my obsessive-compulsive personality is contingent on following this practice. It isn't easy. I also need to avoid the pitfalls of scrupulous behavior. If the impact of my conduct truly bothers me, then making amends is in order. On the other hand, as the sense of inadequacy is lifted from me, I find that much of my way of acting is really okay.

Sayings of the Sages

Bless those who curse you, pray for those who mistreat you.
—Luke 6:28

Live in joy, in peace, even among the troubled.
—Dhammapada, 15

A Hunk of Healing Humor

Love thy neighbor as thyself, but choose your neighborhood.
—Louise Beal

Daily Affirmation

I am being compassionate today.

Twelve Step Thought

It wasn't that hard to list those persons who had suffered somehow from my obsessive-compulsive misdirections. For me, the tough part was reaching a mind-state in which I could admit the damage done. Surely, I knew which friends had been battered by my belligerence or pestered by my rescue-me requests. Following the advice of fellow recovering persons, and after many recitations of the Serenity Prayer, I felt able to turn loose friends and family members who had since died. As for a former spouse and children, an inevitable break has still left behind misunderstanding, financial support owed, and much resentment. Parents were disowned. With my attitude adjusted, the facts readily appeared.

Sayings of the Sages

We have sinned. Do with us as you think fit; only do rescue us today.
   —*Judges 10:15*

Jesus began to be deeply distressed and troubled . . . he fell to the ground and prayed that if possible the hour might pass away from him. . . . "Father," he said, "everything is possible for you. Take this cup from me. Yet not what I will, but what you will."
   —*Mark 14:33, 35 & 36*

A Hunk of Healing Humor

I just read of a new car dealer who raffled off a church!
   —*Robert Orben*

Daily Affirmation

I accept my mistakes and I'm open to corrective action.

Twelve Step Thought

Step Four focused on *my* faults. Step Eight zeroed in on the *damage* I had done to *others*. Admitting that I had hurt other people was a much more difficult proposition. As if that wasn't enough, I was being advised that I should become willing to make amends to *all* persons I had harmed! I found the mandates of this principle to be utterly gut-wrenching. And the requirement of absolute honesty in this matter filled me with fear. To begin with, I was inordinately afraid of confrontation. For me, the discipline demanded by this Step seemed like being condemned to face a firing squad. But I knew H.P. would help me be willing.

Sayings of the Sages

Will you not learn the lesson and listen to my words?
    —*Jeremiah 35:13*

In those days, John the Baptist came, preaching in the desert of Judea and saying, "Repent, for the kingdom of heaven is near." Confessing their sins, they were baptized by him.
    —*Matthew 3:1, 2 & 6*

A Hunk of Healing Humor

I don't want any yes-men around me. I want everybody to tell me the truth even if it costs them their jobs.
    —*Samuel Goldwyn*

Daily Affirmation

For those I've hurt, I'm willing to make amends.

Twelve Step Thought

Going beyond my anger and resentments is being willing to make amends to those I have harmed. Yet, worrying about the possible negative reactions of others reduces my willingness. For me, it's like the fear of being lost at sea in a dense fog. I simply can't control such a situation! Similarly, I'm unable to predict how others will receive my gesture. I'm afraid of sinking— my hull being punctured by the sharp-rock shoals of others' resistance. Once again, I must trust a hardly known Force to help me through.

Sayings of the Sages

First go and be reconciled to your brother, then come and offer your gift.
    —*Matthew 5:24*

Set things in order before there is confusion.
    —*Tao Te Ching, 64*

A Hunk of Healing Humor

Most people agree with the person who keeps his mouth shut.
    —*Anonymous*

Daily Affirmation

The Force is with me today.

Twelve Step Thought

Oh, how I resisted the Eighth Step! I was deathly afraid of it ripping apart my life. A senseless fear possessed me. I ran away from this principle, as if saving what remained of me depended on my finding refuge elsewhere. For a while, I escaped a solution that I sorely needed. Fortunately, my Higher Power was wiser than I. It acted on this matter in its own time. It got my attention by hitting me up the side of the head with the "club" of severe mental conflict and emotional trauma. I realized that the moment for making a list had arrived.

Sayings of the Sages

He alloweth every man to do and leave undone according to his will, whether it be good or bad, and resisteth none.
—*Theologia Germanica, XXXIII*

If anyone sins and . . . does one of the things forbidden by God's commandments, he must answer for it.
—*Leviticus 5:17*

A Hunk of Healing Humor

Some people have psychoceramic personalities. They're crackpots.
—*David de Chiron*

Daily Affirmation

I'm benefitting from my Higher Power's wisdom.

Twelve Step Thought

Once again, a Higher Power used pain as a key to unlock my resistance. Now ready for list making, I sought a sponsor's help to support me as I gazed back into my past. To the best of my ability *at that time* I surveyed the human wreckage on the trail behind me. (Some of it was me.) I intensified efforts to truly discover how many and which people I had harmed. Also, I tried to determine in what ways I had hurt them. There I was compiling a list of those I had pained in some fashion. Very quickly, I began benefiting from my surrender and acceptance. All this, due to God's loving grace.

Sayings of the Sages

If a man or a woman commits any of the sins by which men break faith with God, that person incurs guilt. He must confess the sin he has committed and restore in full the amount for which he is liable.
    —*Numbers 5:6 & 7*

Unless you repent, you too will all perish.
    —*Luke 13:3*

A Hunk of Healing Humor

There are several good protections against temptation, but the surest is cowardice.
    —*Mark Twain*

Daily Affirmation

God's loving grace is unlocking my resistance.

Twelve Step Thought

While laying out the list of those I had harmed, my little ego tried to escape from reviewing some of the wrongs I had done. A marvelous mental mechanism came into play: selective memory. It seems there were some details I just couldn't remember. How convenient! You don't have to deal with something that you've forgotten. So, for a while, certain facts were held in suspension in a sort of psychic limbo. However, a dear friend who knew me well helped me regain awareness of these facts. And, with a Higher Power's help, I did face them.

Sayings of the Sages

Sometimes we are hesitant, sometimes underhanded, and sometimes secretive. Little fears cause anxiety, and great fears cause panic.
—*Chuang Tsu: Inner Chapters, 2*

They were startled and frightened. . . . He said to them, "Why are you troubled, and why do doubts rise in your minds?"
—*Luke 24:37 & 38*

A Hunk of Healing Humor

When a man's dog turns against him it is time for a wife to pack her trunk and go home to mama.
—*Mark Twain*

Daily Affirmation

H.P. helps me face the wrongs I've done.

Twelve Step Thought

In seeking further escape, my fertile imagination fixated on wrongs done to me. Resentment became another route I attempted as an end-run around my responsibility for surveying the more sordid wreckage of my past. Rather than face the music, I chose a form of mental masturbation for supposed relief. After all, the reopening of certain old emotional wounds seemed like a purposeless piece of surgery. And I can't stomach the sight of blood! Over time, writing the list in my personal journal reduced the threat and the seeming purposelessness. Then, I accepted my part in the *whole* mess.

Sayings of the Sages

Repent, then, and turn to God, so that your sins may be wiped out, that times of refreshing may come.
    —*Acts 3:19 & 20*

Do not be afraid, for I am with you; stop being anxious and watchful, for I am your God.
    —*Isaiah 41:10*

A Hunk of Healing Humor

Let us be thankful for the fools; but for them the rest of us could not succeed.
    —*Mark Twain*

Daily Affirmation

Today, I accept responsibility for my faults.

Twelve Step Thought

Wading ever further into recovery, I found myself wagering everything on a new approach to life. So, in writing down a list of people I had harmed, I also was avoiding a resentful attitude which could defeat my purpose. No longer could I conveniently "forget" my misbehaviors, nor could I minimize my role in the messed-up relationships scattered along the path behind me. By trying my best to build honest and loving communicating into my life, I was betting that any obstacles to my new existence would melt away. The main advantage of carrying out this step was the peace seeping into my soul.

Sayings of the Sages

I want you to take care of yourself, because next time I see you I want to talk *to* you, not *about* you. And when I no longer have to talk to you, I want to be able to talk about you, for the edification of others.
    —*Idries Shah, Reflections*

Then I saw a new heaven and a new earth.
    —*Revelation 21:1*

A Hunk of Healing Humor

There is one way to find out if a man is honest—ask him. If he says "yes," you know he is crooked.
    —*Groucho Marx*

Daily Affirmation

I'm honest and loving in dealing with others.

Twelve Step Thought

The spirit of reconciliation dominates Step Eight. *The American Heritage Dictionary* defines *reconcile* as follows: "1. To re-establish friendship between. 2. To settle or resolve, as a dispute. 3. To bring to acquiescence: *reconcile oneself to defeat.* 4. To make compatible or consistent." In my case, becoming reconciled meant to reestablish friendship between *me* and *I*; it implied being willing to resolve any disputes with others; and it signified becoming compatible with my new way of life. In honestly practicing this principle, I even learned to avoid extreme judgments of others and myself.

Sayings of the Sages

Save yourselves from this corrupt generation.
  —*Acts 2:40*

Be firmly fixed in purity, not caring for acquisition and preservation, and be possessed of the Self.
  —*Bhagavad Gita II, 45*

A Hunk of Healing Humor

Acquaintance: a degree of friendship called slight when its object is poor or obscure, and intimate when he is rich and famous.
  —*Ambrose Bierce*

Daily Affirmation

I'm avoiding judging others or myself.

Twelve Step Thought

After a careful and willing survey, which followed many hesitations, I did recall all those I had offended. Yet, I also remembered that obsessive and addictive personalities are not the only ones bothered by twisted emotions. When I was actively practicing my addiction, my dysfunctional behavior sometimes just worsened the already existing defects of others. To be around me at all in the dark days of my illness, those close to me had to be as sick as I was. For years, almost no healthy communication took place. Now, the supportive voice of my Higher Power helps me to claim my rightful share in the sickness of unhealthy relationships.

Sayings of the Sages

An untroubled mind, no longer seeking to consider what is right and what is wrong, a mind beyond judgments, watches and understands.

—*Dhammapada, 3*

Evil spirits came out of many, and many ... were healed.

—*Acts 8:7*

A Hunk of Healing Humor

If you keep your mind sufficiently open, people will throw a lot of rubbish into it.

—*William A. Orton*

Daily Affirmation

My Higher Power is helping me be honest about relationships.

Twelve Step Thought

As I prepare to ask forgiveness from others for the wrongs I committed, it's entirely appropriate that I begin this process by forgiving others. This means *everyone* I feel has wronged me. Yet, in truth, I feel overwhelmed by the prospect of extending forgiveness to my worst enemies. Even scarier is the notion of telling these persons how sorry I am for the harm I did to them. Still, I know and accept that, when I forgive whomever, I fulfill a basic prerequisite of Step Eight. Such "footwork" constitutes a vital part of becoming willing to make amends to all those I had harmed.

Sayings of the Sages

We never perceive our sins until we begin to cure them.
    —*Vernon Howard*

The virtuous man must be kindly to his fellow men.
    —*Wisdom 12:19*

A Hunk of Healing Humor

Every man is a damn fool for at least five minutes every day; wisdom consists in not exceeding the limit.
    —*Elbert Hubbard*

Daily Affirmation

Today, I forgive everyone who has wronged me.

Twelve Step Thought

In reviewing those I had harmed during my obsessive illness, an unexpected question arose in my mind. Some people are still not aware that I have hurt them. What should I do about them? Isn't it better to leave well enough alone? If so, I shouldn't append their names to my amends list. However, then I would be making an exception to the willingness which I claimed to possess. That really would be skirting the truth by keeping my mouth shut. In other words, I would be lying through omission. Even worse, I would be pretending my offense never happened. I can no longer live so deceitfully!

Sayings of the Sages

Using the outer light, return to insight, and in this way be saved from harm. This is learning constancy.
　　—*Tao Te Ching, 52*

Every word of God is unalloyed. . . . To his words make no addition, lest he reprove you and know you for a fraud.
　　—*Proverbs 30:5 & 6*

A Hunk of Healing Humor

One toothpaste manufacturer has something that's guaranteed to remove film. Wouldn't it be wonderful if TV bought some?
　　—*Robert Orben*

Daily Affirmation

I'm living truthfully today.

Twelve Step Thought

For a while I remained indifferent to the making of amends. I now understand that this indifference stemmed from having reservations about the spiritual side of my sickness. Once again a paradoxical aspect of addiction besieged me: If I truly suffered from a serious illness, why am I morally responsible for making restitution for things I did during addictive binges? For now, I'm relying on the assurances of those who successfully worked this step before me. And, as for all confusion, I turn to my Higher Power for guidance.

Sayings of the Sages

Neither may a man, who is made a partaker of the divine nature, oppress or grieve any one. It never entereth into his thoughts, or intents, or wishes, to cause pain or distress to any, either by deed or neglect, by speech or silence.
    —*Theologia Germanica, XXXIII*

I came into the world to testify to the truth.
    —*John 18:37*

A Hunk of Healing Humor

Most of our future lies ahead.
    —*Denny Crum, Louisville basketball coach*

Daily Affirmation

I'm guided by my Higher Power in all that I do.

Twelve Step Thought

While living in recovery, I prepared to correct past errors and to make restitution to those I wronged. Gradually, I increased my willingness for righting relationships that had been turned upside down by my compulsive behavior. While putting together a list, I continued to pursue my new existence as a recovering person. So, while I worked on Step Eight, I practiced almost all the rest of the Twelve Steps. I took a daily personal inventory. I remembered I'm generally powerless without a Higher Power. I prayed and meditated. I asked my Higher Power to remove my shortcomings. I carried the message. Trusting it would restore me, I turned my will over to my Higher Power on a daily basis.

Sayings of the Sages

Let us wake in the morning filled with your love and sing and be happy all our days.
    —*Psalm 90:14*

One who hurts others will in turn be hurt. Using the failings of others to demonstrate your own superiority is deliberately hurting other people.
    —*Chuang Tsu: Inner Chapters, 4*

A Hunk of Healing Humor

Except when I'm wrong, I'm always right.
    —*William Roylance*

Daily Affirmation

Each day in recovery is filled with God's love.

Twelve Step Thought

In thinking over hurts I perpetrated, I realized there were some instances where no significant harm was done to others. However, in those cases, the emotional harm I did to myself was tremendous. In fact, for every situation, a major part of the damage was done to myself. Without a doubt, I had been in process of wrecking my physical health. Also, I all but ripped apart my feelings. I worried almost constantly; and I stressed my mind beyond all normal endurance. The very atmosphere of my soul was sickened to the point where I preferred death on a few occasions. For me, a vital component of this self-examination was a search for clues to ensure the salvaging of my whole being.

Sayings of the Sages

The Lord abides in the hearts of all beings.
    —*Bhagavad Gita XVIII, 61*

We know that anyone born of God does not continue to sin; the one who was born of God keeps him safe.
    —*I John 5:18*

A Hunk of Healing Humor

It is by the goodness of God that in our country we have those three unspeakably precious things: freedom of speech, freedom of conscience, and the prudence never to practice either.
    —*Mark Twain*

Daily Affirmation

I am learning the lessons I need to become whole.

Twelve Step Thought

I've been told that the principal facet of Step Eight is self-examination geared to making restitution to those wronged. Yet, along the way, I found out it was just as important that I really learn what makes me tick—especially in relating to other people. In fact, it became essential that I extricate from this examining process all possible information about myself and about my seemingly inherent difficulties with personal relations. In addition, I did discover my fundamental fear: that people would find out how inadequate I truly was. And I greatly feared confrontation with others. Now, I plan to make amends to others and to myself.

Sayings of the Sages

The reasonings of mortals are unsure and our intentions unstable; for a perishable body presses down the soul.
      —*Wisdom 9:14 & 15*

Humble knowledge of self is a surer path to God than the ardent pursuit of learning.
      —*The Imitation of Christ I, 3*

A Hunk of Healing Humor

Everybody gets so much common information all day long that they lose their common sense.
      —*Gertrude Stein*

Daily Affirmation

I'm learning about me and about relating better to others.

Twelve Step Thought

Appropriately making contact with others had been a long-standing problem with me. I experienced a lot of difficulties with honest communication. Yet, a new door gradually opened for me. Step Eight began the ending of isolation from my fellows and from God. It was also the launching pad that propelled me to a whole different level of communicating with my fellow humans. Willingness to make amends evolved into willingness to *talk with* others. Eventually, "talking with" included being more open, going with the flow, risking constructive criticism—as well as asking for and giving feedback.

Sayings of the Sages

He who is equal-minded among friends, companions and foes, among those who are neutral and impartial, among those who are related or indifferent to him, among saints and sinners, he excels.
—*Bhagavad Gita VI, 9*

All of them were filled with the Holy Spirit and began to speak in other languages as the Spirit enabled them.
—*Acts 2:4*

A Hunk of Healing Humor

When I think over what I have said, I envy dumb people.
—*Seneca*

Daily Affirmation

I'm making contact honestly with everyone I meet.

Twelve Step Thought

In making a list of people I had hurt, I more deeply experienced the reality that there are no perfect relationships. My addictive extremism and perfectionism had me convinced that I should easily relate to all persons at all times. Needless to say, the real world did not bear out that conviction! Yet, being an obsessive and stubborn individual, I ran head-first into the proverbial brick wall quite a few more times before I accepted the realities of relating to others without any reservations. In looking back, I guess I needed to develop a willingness to more and more accept people as they are.

Sayings of the Sages

Whoever is not against you is for you.
    —*Luke 9:50*

You may give in the spirit of light or as you please; but if you care how another man gives or how he withholds, you trouble your quietness endlessly.
    —*Dhammapada, 18*

A Hunk of Healing Humor

I'd like to get married because I like the idea of a man being required by law to sleep with me every night.
    —*Carrie Snow*

Daily Affirmation

I'm accepting people I encounter as they are.

Twelve Step Thought

As I recalled how I had harmed others, I discovered that they and I were hurt by my negative emotional conflicts. Viewing the scene with hindsight, I know that anger and resentment were my most dangerous feelings. Since I didn't like to look at them, I often "stuffed" such uncomfortable feelings. Thus, some twisted emotions persisted for a very long time at an unconscious level. I now believe that I suffered most from the garbage which was rotting just below the level of consciousness. Given this understanding, reworking Step Eight makes a lot of sense.

Sayings of the Sages

Man's wrath only adds to your glory; the survivors of your wrath you will draw like a girdle around you.
—*Psalm 76:10*

After a bitter quarrel, some resentment must remain. What can one do about it? Therefore the sage keeps his half of the bargain but does not exact his due.
—*Tao Te Ching, 79*

A Hunk of Healing Humor

My mother had a great deal of trouble with me, but I think she enjoyed it.
—*Mark Twain*

Daily Affirmation

I'm relying on a Higher Power to remove my negativities.

Twelve Step Thought

In pursuing a pre-amends listing of those I had harmed, I made some interesting discoveries about my behavior patterns. The manner in which I pained people seemed to reflect the methods by which I felt hurt in my younger years. My feelings had been flayed by the angry silent treatment; I manifested my anger by giving persons close to me the silent treatment. Having been put down when attempting to share my feelings, I put down others trying to share their feelings with me. As I had been made to feel inadequate, I—quite sarcastically and with a vengeance—at times caused others to feel inadequate. Now, however, the desire for greater growth means I'm changing my old ways.

Sayings of the Sages

The nearer a man cometh thereunto [being a partaker of the divine nature], and the more godlike and divine he becometh, the more he hateth all disobedience, sin, evil and unrighteousness, and the worse they grieve him.
—*Theologia Germanica, XVI*

A Hunk of Healing Humor

Don't give me advice, give me money.
—*Spanish proverb*

Daily Affirmation

I'm changing my old ways so I can grow more.

Twelve Step Thought

After being in recovery for a few years, I realized that I really *need* to make more headway in the adventure of living. Either I keep moving ahead or I stagnate and lose ground. Finally, I seriously approached and practiced Step Eight. I wholeheartedly made an honest start on working this step. And the benefits of practicing the step soon revealed themselves to me. I began to experience a significant spurt of personal growth. I gradually gained great insights into my patterns of thinking, feeling, and acting. Happily, my Higher Power helped me apply the lessons of these revelations in my daily life.

Sayings of the Sages

Men cannot see their reflection in running water but only in still water. Only that which is still in itself can still the seekers of stillness.
　　—*Chuang Tsu: Inner Chapters, 5*

To him who is thirsty I will give freely from the well of the water of life.
　　—*Revelation 21:6*

A Hunk of Healing Humor

The right to be heard does not automatically include the right to be taken seriously.
　　—*Hubert Humphrey*

Daily Affirmation

My Higher Power is helping me apply the lessons I'm learning.

Twelve Step Thought

Disturbed feelings, stuck at an unconscious level, generated a lot of stress in my conscious life. Stress frequently served as the immediate cause of my practicing my addiction. Thus, I needed to find ways to reduce the degree of stress in my life. Working with a therapist assisted me in uncovering negative emotions buried deep in my unconscious. Also, writing in my personal journal gradually put me in touch with previously unknown aspects of my character. Finally, doing progressive relaxation every day—as well as praying and meditating—diminished the sting of the stressors in my life.

Sayings of the Sages

Be all the more eager to make your calling and election sure. For, if you do these things, you will never fall.
　　—II Peter 1:10

Talking about straws and camels' backs is just one way of approaching things. If you have enough camels, no backs need be broken.
　　—Idries Shah, Reflections

A Hunk of Healing Humor

A conclusion is the place where you got tired of thinking.
　　—Arthur Bloch

Daily Affirmation

I'm shedding negative feelings and excess stress from my life.

Twelve Step Thought

In sincerely working Step Eight, I acquired the awareness and understanding of my life patterns that were
necessary to prevent relapse. After all, I had already
learned (the hard way) a closely related lesson: I couldn't
just agree with the principles of the Twelve Steps;
rather, I actually needed to live them. It's not a question
of semantics. *Practicing* these principles in all that I do
is essential to my survival in recovery. Practice may
not readily make me perfect; but it certainly does make
me better. So I went into action to deal with the
negative patterns that weighed down my life. With the
grace of my Higher Power, new positive patterns are
forming over the old negative ones.

Sayings of the Sages

The master comes out from behind his ignorance.
  —*Dhammapada, 13*

Jesus looked at them and said, "With man this is
impossible, but with God all things are possible."
  —*Matthew 19:26*

A Hunk of Healing Humor

The mode by which the inevitable comes to pass is
effort.
  —*Oliver Wendell Holmes*

Daily Affirmation

Practicing Twelve Step principles is making me better.

Twelve Step Thought

For me, becoming willing to make amends involved repenting. *The American Heritage Dictionary* defines *repent* as follows: "1. To feel remorse or self-reproach for what one has done or failed to do. 2. To feel such remorse or regret for past conduct as to change one's mind regarding it. 3. To feel remorse or contrition for one's sins and to abjure sinful ways." Furthermore, this dictionary defines *remorse* as "moral anguish arising from . . . past misdeeds." So the building of willingness is really meant to relieve *my* emotional and mental hurt over past treatment of others. Who knows if it will help them? Now I understand that such planned amends are designed for achieving my peace of mind.

Sayings of the Sages

Repent and be baptized, every one of you . . . so that your sins may be forgiven. And you will receive the gift of the Holy Spirit.
  —*Acts 2:38*

He unto whom all desires enter as waters into the sea, which, though ever being filled is ever motionless, attains to peace and not he who hugs his desires.
  —*Bhagavad Gita II, 70*

A Hunk of Healing Humor

We don't seem to be able to check crime, so why not legalize it and then tax it out of business?
  —*Will Rogers*

Daily Affirmation

My list-making and willingness are relieving my inner pain.

Twelve Step Thought

As I'm pursuing this new way of life, I expect to receive forgiveness and tolerance from others. After all, I'm trying so hard to be a good recovering person. Therefore, why shouldn't others forgive me and tolerate my idiosyncrasies? I deserve it! Yet, I wonder if I always respond in kind when the shoe is on the other foot. Am I truly open to forgiving and tolerating others? Am I willing to make amends to people I've hurt by my past conduct? Perhaps the more basic question is, can and do I extend the same consideration that I fully anticipate getting from others? If not, I'm apt to drown in the depths of egocentricity.

Sayings of the Sages

I am good to people who are good. I am also good to people who are not good. Because Virtue is goodness.
   —*Tao Te Ching, 49*

Jesus said, "Father, forgive them, for they do not know what they are doing."
   —*Luke 23:34*

A Hunk of Healing Humor

Do you realize it only took six days to create the world? Just shows you what can be done if you don't take coffee breaks!
   —*Robert Orben*

Daily Affirmation

Today, I'm being good to everyone I meet.

Twelve Step Thought

By living this personal growth Program as well as I could, I already had begun making amends to myself. This course promoted "selfishness" in a very positive and realistic sense. In truth, I had all but destroyed myself at the high point of my illness. So I sought reconciliation with myself: with my outraged body, with my warped emotions, with my confused mind, and with my troubled spirit. This was an honest ordering of priorities, since I had harmed myself most of all. By letting go of my old harmful ways, I rightfully was being considerate to a very damaged me. Then, I felt secure enough, with God's grace, for extending consideration to others I had hurt.

Sayings of the Sages

I will make the blind walk along the road and lead them along paths. I will turn darkness into light before them and rocky places into level tracks.
—*Isaiah 42:16*

You shall be free indeed when your days are not without a care nor your nights without a want and a grief, but rather when these things girdle your life and yet you rise above them naked and unbound.
—*Kahlil Gibran*

A Hunk of Healing Humor

Never play leapfrog with a unicorn.
—*Anonymous*

Daily Affirmation

Today, I'm being considerate to myself and to others.

Twelve Step Thought

As time rolled on in recovery, I realized in how many areas (beyond my principal illness) I was beset by obsessiveness. For example, had I insulted others or caused lung damage through my thoughtless chimney-like practice of smoking three packs of cigarettes daily? Should my listing of persons harmed really extend that far? I retreated to the sanctuary of my conscience. I sought an answer in meditation. I listened most carefully for the still, small voice within. I wrote about it in my journal. Finally, I decided to restrict my assessing to a few obsessive-compulsive disorders and their consequences.

Sayings of the Sages

Some, driven frantic by their sins, made miserable by their own guilt ... were nearly at death's door. Then they called to God in their trouble and he rescued them from their sufferings.
    —Psalm 107:17-19

How can a troubled mind understand the way? If a man is disturbed, he will never be filled with knowledge.
    —Dhammapada, 3

A Hunk of Healing Humor

As Miss America, my goal is to bring peace to the entire world and then to get my own apartment.
    —Jay Leno

Daily Affirmation

I seek the answers I need deep within my soul.

Twelve Step Thought

During the active phase of my illness, I left behind me a number of twisted and broken relationships. At times, I felt very paranoid about these situations. My emotional state turned into anxiety and defensiveness whenever I thought about them. Residual anger made it hard to review such scenes objectively. Yet, they were essential to the pre-amends process I had undertaken. Despite my anguish, I needed to consider them—but not alone, never alone. When isolated, I was likely to fail. So I talked with my sponsor about how I felt. When my sponsor couldn't provide relief, I contacted my therapist. When all assistance seemed useless, I turned it over to H.P., attended meetings, and prayed.

Sayings of the Sages

I have been holding forth on matters I cannot understand, on marvels beyond me and my knowledge. I knew you then only by hearsay; but now, having seen you with my own eyes, I retract all I have said, and . . . I repent.

>   —*Job 42:3-6*

A Hunk of Healing Humor

Don't jump on a man unless he's down.
>   —*Finley Peter Dunne*

Daily Affirmation

I never have to face anything alone anymore.

Twelve Step Thought

Time is often viewed as a nasty four-letter word. Yet, it does resolve all issues. Eventually, given time, I did carry out this pre-amends list, writing with total thoroughness. To the best of my ability, I recalled all the persons I harmed. Also, despite an occasional knot in my gut, I expanded my willingness for making amends to embrace them all. Of course, I accomplished this with a lot of help. For one thing, I attended hundreds of mutual-help meetings. I garnered the example and support of my peers in recovery. I listened to my sponsor as well as to my counselor. I prayed to my Higher Power.

Sayings of the Sages

If right is indeed right, there need be no argument about how it is different from wrong.
    —*Chuang Tsu: Inner Chapters, 2*

Carry each other's burdens. . . . If anyone thinks he is something when he is nothing, he deceives himself. Each man should test his own actions . . . each man should carry his own load.
    —*Galatians 6:2-5*

A Hunk of Healing Humor

There are only two ways of telling the complete truth—anonymously and posthumously.
    —*Thomas Sowell*

Daily Affirmation

I'm being totally thorough about checking out what amends I need to make.

Twelve Step Thought

I experienced quite a state of shock upon completing the list of everyone I had hurt and building the willingness to express my regret. Why? Because it was time for me to face the music. The moment arrived to gear up for a person-to-person encounter with each individual that I had harmed. The hour was striking for me to walk the walk as well as talk the talk. Suddenly, I now would actually be admitting my previous wretched conduct to each one I had pained. There were no weather delays. The launch window was open. The amends shuttle was ready. It was minus ten, and counting—with all rockets properly "higher powered."

Sayings of the Sages

If, however, I say to a wicked man: You are to die, and he renounces his sins and does what is lawful and right, if he returns pledges, restores what he has stolen ... and stops committing sin—he shall live, and will not die.

—Ezekiel 33:14 & 15

A Hunk of Healing Humor

I have never been hurt by anything I didn't say.
—Calvin Coolidge

Daily Affirmation

I accept all appropriate opportunities to ask forgiveness from others.

Twelve Step Thought

Whenever possible, my mission now encompasses dispensing reparations for the ravages of my compulsive behavior. Previously, those who got in my way were cut with the blade of sarcasm. False pride and procrastination then delayed my making amends to those I hurt deliberately. On some occasions, I was too anxious—following an urge to wax emotional and to resolve everything without thinking of others' feelings. Because timing is so crucial, I seek the guidance of my Higher Power for healing wounds.

Sayings of the Sages

Those who slight My teaching and do not follow it, know them to be blind to all wisdom.
    —*Bhagavad Gita III, 32*

With gentleness overcome anger.
    —*Dhammapada, 17*

A Hunk of Healing Humor

It's easier to forgive an enemy after you've gotten even.
    —*Olin Miller*

Daily Affirmation

My Higher Power helps me make amends.

Twelve Step Thought

From my present perspective, I know that abstinence alone isn't enough. People who proclaim that just being in recovery is enough are definitely inconsiderate. Once I found a foothold in recovery, I then had to face an extended period of reconstruction. After all, it took a long time for me to get as messed up as I was. Rebuilding takes quite a while too. For me, making amends eventually became an integral part of putting my life back together. Along with asking God's grace to right the wrongs, I ventured out to meet with persons I had harmed.

Sayings of the Sages

They who try to overcome the most difficult and unpleasant obstacles far outstrip others in the pursuit of virtue.
—*The Imitation of Christ I, 25*

So now amend your behaviour and actions, listen to the voice of . . . your God.
—*Jeremiah 26:13*

A Hunk of Healing Humor

It is much easier to repent of sins that we have committed than to repent of those that we intend to commit.
—*Josh Billings*

Daily Affirmation

Making amends is part of putting my life together.

Twelve Step Thought

Under no conditions can I afford to live in an angry or resentful mood. My rehabilitation depends upon extending forgiveness and making amends. Today, I can expiate uncounted past misdeeds by more readily forgiving those who seem to hurt me. Whenever possible, I seek healthier relationships with the victims (especially myself) of my insane obsession. To be truly whole, I must focus on clearing away blame. And, when compulsive cyclones are stirred by erratic biochemical windstreams, I must turn to the One that calms all storms.

Sayings of the Sages

Above all, love each other deeply, because love covers over a multitude of sins.
   —*I Peter 4:8*

In dealing with others, be gentle and kind.
   —*Tao Te Ching, 8*

A Hunk of Healing Humor

Instead of loving your enemies, treat your friends a little better.
   —*Ed Howe*

Daily Affirmation

I walk safely through stormy weather.

Twelve Step Thought

Once I finished Step Eight in the presence of my sponsor, I set out to work the Ninth Step. It truly was time for me to clean house. In each major instance, I first sought strength from the unconditionally loving Deity. I ardently asked that I be shown the way of patience, tolerance, egolessness, kindliness, and love. In fact, I soon discovered that I couldn't make an amend that wasn't preceded by prayer and meditation. Otherwise, it seemed like a particular amend lacked in fullness of purpose and effectiveness. Deep down, I wanted to proceed according to my Guide's sense of timing rather than my ego's chancy schedule.

Sayings of the Sages

Enthusiasm is the greatest asset in the world. It beats money and power and influence.
    —*Henry Chester*

The heavens declare the glory of God, the vault of heaven proclaims his handiwork; day discourses of it to day, night to night hands on the knowledge.
    —*Psalm 19:1 & 2*

A Hunk of Healing Humor

The first half of our lives is ruined by our parents and the second half by our children.
    —*Clarence Darrow*

Daily Affirmation

I'm being guided in all my amends by prayer and meditation.

Twelve Step Thought

What was recommended to me for practicing Step Nine was in-person contact with persons I had harmed. Both my sponsor and support group peers strongly suggested that the face-to-face approach was the preferred method for seeking amends. The one qualifier is "wherever possible." In some instances, death or comparable unfavorable circumstances prevented any physical proximity. Long-distance confession is somewhat problematic. Apologizing to people who resided on the East Coast proved difficult when I lived on the West Coast. Besides actual presence being "nicer," there seems to be a mental and physical need for vibrational contact with my victims to facilitate internal admission and absolution.

Sayings of the Sages

Our words fly off like arrows, as though we knew what was right and wrong. We cling to our own point of view, as though everything depended on it. And yet our opinions have no permanence: like autumn and winter, they gradually pass away.
— *Chuang Tsu: Inner Chapters, 2*

A Hunk of Healing Humor

The worst thing in this world, next to anarchy, is government.
— *Henry Ward Beecher*

Daily Affirmation

Whenever possible, I make direct amends to those I hurt.

Twelve Step Thought

My whole amends process proceeded in stages. It was
initiated through writing letters, this being my favored
medium of communication. Much time passed before I
reached the next plateau. Then, I was able to telephone
the principal parties to whom I owed apologies. There
was a long session with my sponsor and much praying
immediately prior to this series of phone calls. After
calling, I felt very relieved. The next level involved
personal visits. I undertook a few long trips for this
purpose. This finally produced a great resolution of the
guilt and paranoia within me.

Sayings of the Sages

The wise man's heart leads him aright, the fool's heart
leads him astray.
  —*Ecclesiastes 10:2*

With a cosmic conscience we see that anything done
against others is also done against ourselves.
  —*Vernon Howard*

A Hunk of Healing Humor

What ought to be done to the man who invented the
celebrating of anniversaries? Mere killing would be too
light.
  —*Mark Twain*

Daily Affirmation

My heart and my Higher Power are leading me in the
right direction.

Twelve Step Thought

Some of my atonement involved legalities. Here practicality led to acquiring an attorney who understood my position in recovery. I needed to face the long-term residuals of prior messes I had made. Matters such as past-due payments had to be addressed. Somehow the legal system isn't set up to be impressed by remorse or apologies. It is geared to guaranteeing that legally mandated obligations are met. Although I wasn't thrilled by the drama of straightening out this area of my life, I did feel honest and clean. On the brighter side, while some were in prison, I was free, thanks to H.P.

Sayings of the Sages

The children of God ... whom temporal things do not so attract that they cling to them, but who rather put these things to such proper service as is ordained and instituted by God.
—The Imitation of Christ III, 38

We are not trying to please men but God, who tests our hearts.
—I Thessalonians 2:4

A Hunk of Healing Humor

Do you ever get the feeling that the only reason we have elections is to find out if the polls were right?
—Robert Orben

Daily Affirmation

I am pleasing God in straightening out my life.

Twelve Step Thought

By preparing myself as much as possible in advance, I didn't let cold or skeptical reactions deter me from my course of proffering appropriate reconciliation. As with my letters, with my in-person visits I tried to emphasize honesty and avoid expressions of anger or resentment. Nevertheless, I found great pain in this process. A special person whom I had always loved very much remained silent and invisible, refusing to communicate with me. This heartache became part of the expiation I had to experience to balance the harm my sickness had occasioned for others. So I learned anew that joy and tears can co-exist in my heart.

Sayings of the Sages

Sometimes we go through very difficult phases [in personal growth]. This is really good because it helps us appreciate what the guru [i.e., spiritual teacher] has given us when things work out for the better.
　　—*Nityanadaji*

A Hunk of Healing Humor

I believe in the discipline of silence and could talk for hours about it.
　　—*George Bernard Shaw*

Daily Affirmation

Joy and tears co-exist in my heart which is seeking God.

Twelve Step Thought

Friends in recovery suggested that I not attempt atonement with any persons who were still smarting from a recent impropriety inflicted by me. It appears that a cooling-off period constitutes one necessary aspect of this amends process. When the other party yet burns the fuel of her or his initial anger or resentment, the flames aren't ready to be extinguished. When the fire fodder is used up, then is the moment for the amender to seek a harmonious resolution. My own experience definitely confirms this sage advice. I remained unable to connect with the hurt individual's intellect and spirit when an impenetrable fence of fiery feelings blocked the way.

Sayings of the Sages

There is no fire like passion, there are no chains like hate. Illusion is a net, desire a rushing river.
  —*Dhammapada, 18*

A mild answer turns away wrath, sharp words stir up anger. The tongue of wise men makes pleasing knowledge, the mouth of fools spews folly.
  —*Proverbs 15:1 & 2*

A Hunk of Healing Humor

The world is divided into two classes—invalids and nurses.
  —*James McNeill Whistler*

Daily Affirmation

I'm wisely watching the timing of my amends.

Twelve Step Thought

My ongoing and eventually full recovery depends on the making of amends. This is a lifelong commitment for me. The admitting and rectifying of wrongs constitute a regenerative process vital to my successful rehabilitation. It forms a new openness to the true, the humble, the beautiful, and the good which characterizes one who is reborn. It's a resolving of my karmic predicament, wherein I had become a person perpetually haunted by past negative acts. Confession and reparation tend to liberate me from this vicious cycle. Aided by these mediating mechanisms and transformed by the saving grace of my Higher Power, I'm getting off the merry-go-round.

Sayings of the Sages

Thus shalt thou be freed from the good and evil results which are the bonds of action . . . thou shalt become free and attain to Me.
   —*Bhagavad Gita IX, 28*

Blessed are the peacemakers, for they will be called sons of God. Blessed are those who are persecuted because of righteousness, for theirs is the kingdom of heaven.
   —*Matthew 5:9 & 10*

A Hunk of Healing Humor

Lord Ronald said nothing; he flung himself from the room, flung himself upon his horse and rode madly off in all directions.
   —*Stephen Leacock*

Daily Affirmation

I'm becoming liberated from the vicious cycle of negative actions.

Twelve Step Thought

In seriously pursuing the path of personal wholeness, I realized the need for expiating my past misdeeds. I must confess, too: I did procrastinate. I let myself seem stuck in my special set of conditions. All the while, I prayed and meditated. Feeling crushed under the weight of my dilemmas, I finally sought a definitive release. My meditations occurred daily. Then, I was blessed with total willingness to make amends as fast and as far as I possibly could. Now being zealous, I sought the helpful advice of my sponsor rather than inadvertently injure someone by a hasty expression of regret. After I checked it out, H.P. rocketed me into reconciliation.

Sayings of the Sages

"Do to others as you would have them do to you" . . . was originally intended to make people think. They were expected to react by asking why it should be a good policy, considering that most people want the wrong things for themselves.
    —*Idries Shah, Reflections*

A Hunk of Healing Humor

If people don't want to come out to the ball park, nobody's going to stop them.
    —*Yogi Berra*

Daily Affirmation

H.P. blesses me with total willingness to make any and all amends.

Twelve Step Thought

One day I went to those I had harmed, asking forgiveness and offering my amends. I strived to proffer amends in a straightforward and generous manner, without wallowing in excessive remorse. Following friendly suggestions of Twelve Steppers, I tried my utmost to behave sensibly and tactfully and considerately and humbly. I strictly avoided acting in a servile or scraping fashion. Since accepting myself as one of God's children, I rightfully could stand on both feet. I no longer had to crawl before anyone. That sort of attitude would only injure me. I haven't the right to hurt myself any more than I do to harm others. H.P. is really healing me.

Sayings of the Sages

Unless your righteousness surpasses that of the Pharisees and the teachers of the law, you will certainly not enter the kingdom of heaven.
    —*Matthew 5:20*

He who conceals his faults will not prosper, he who confesses and renounces them will find mercy.
    —*Proverbs 28:13*

A Hunk of Healing Humor

When you have got an elephant by the hind legs and he is trying to run away, it is best to let him.
    —*Abraham Lincoln*

Daily Affirmation

I ask forgiveness while standing tall as a child of God.

Twelve Step Thought

Practicing the Twelve Steps is a proven way of life. On this course, the obsessive and addictive person corrects prior mistakes and provides reasonable restitution. Many generations of Twelve Steppers have preceded me on this path. The recent ones taught me that *making amends* means much more than saying I'm sorry. I learned that the basic spirit of Step Nine involves the readiness to accept the full consequences of my past actions. Also, I'm told, this step includes responsibility for the well-being of others. At times, this step seems like a very, very tall order. Yet, it is part of a well-validated lifestyle which has worked for many others in recovery.

Sayings of the Sages

Tauler [Johannes Tauler, a friend of Meister Eckhart] saith: "there be some men at the present time, who take leave of types and symbols too soon, before they have drawn out all the truth and instruction contained therein." Hence they are scarcely or perhaps never able to understand the truth aright.

    —*Theologia Germanica, XIII*

A Hunk of Healing Humor

Often it does seem a pity that Noah and his party did not miss the boat.

    —*Mark Twain*

Daily Affirmation

I accept the consequences of my actions, and I seek good for others.

Twelve Step Thought

As my illness grew more intense over time, so did the ravages wrought upon my relationships. Generally speaking, my contacts with others suffered from abuse and neglect. More and more, I tended to isolate myself. Much of my limited social life was spent in a sort of numb state. Thus, the damage I did to those close to me took place over a number of years. Then came the salvage and repair job of recovery. A *long* process of change was initiated. Fortunately, I received warm support for my personal development work from some wonderful Twelve Step Programs. Now, I come from my heart in relating to others.

Sayings of the Sages

Teach us to count how few days we have and so gain wisdom of heart.
>   —*Psalm 90:12*

Words are like the wind and the waves; action involves the risk of gain or loss. The wind and the waves are easily set in motion; risk can easily turn into real danger.
>   —*Chuang Tsu: Inner Chapters, 4*

A Hunk of Healing Humor

There is no human problem which could not be solved if people would simply do as I advise.
>   —*Gore Vidal*

Daily Affirmation

I come from my heart in relating to others.

Twelve Step Thought

In my case, Step Nine has restored a few discarded friendships. Various persons in recovery have told me they regained many more previously damaged relationships. That's okay with me, since I never fostered a lot of relationships in the first place. For the most part I had lived as a surface relater. In other words, almost no one was allowed anywhere near the sanctuary of my feelings and my spirit. Somehow, helped along by my Higher Power, a couple of former contacts did blossom anew. How wonderful! And perhaps just a bit more peace and happiness reached a few who had formerly suffered from the symptoms of my obsessiveness and addiction.

Sayings of the Sages

Make our future as happy as our past was sad.
    —*Psalm 90:15*

Anyone who claims to be in the light but hates his brother is still in the darkness. Whoever loves his brother lives in the light, and there is nothing in him to make him stumble.
    —*I John 2:9 & 10*

A Hunk of Healing Humor

I don't make jokes. I just watch the government and report the facts.
    —*Will Rogers*

Daily Affirmation

My Higher Power is causing wonders to blossom in my life.

Twelve Step Thought

In pursuing the reparation of relationships, I sought to avoid a self-centered approach which could have violated the confidentiality rights of another. Prior to starting any action which might infringe on the rights of someone else, I needed to obtain her or his concurrence with my strategy. I learned that I had an obligation to respect the feelings of others. With thornier problems, great discretion was required. Sometimes, good orderly direction indicated that my problem should be attacked on the flank. Otherwise, I risked a frontal assault under very trying circumstances, which is a recipe for relapse.

Sayings of the Sages

If God does not build the house, in vain the masons toil; if God does not guard the city, in vain the sentries watch.
   —*Psalm 127:1*

Grace does not consider what is useful and advantageous to herself, but rather what is profitable to many. Nature likes to receive honor and reverence, but grace faithfully attributes all honor and glory to God.
   —*The Imitation of Christ III, 54*

A Hunk of Healing Humor

To be positive: to be mistaken at the top of one's voice.
   —*Ambrose Bierce*

Daily Affirmation

In pursuing reconciliation, I'm following good orderly direction.

Twelve Step Thought

In the prior acutely sick phase, my prideful self frequently overrated my limited achievements. Similarly, in the earlier recovery phase, my guiltful self bragged excessively about the extent of my defects. Negative pride surfaced quite diabolically. At Twelve Step meetings, I admitted all my mistakes ad nauseam. To enhance my story, I even invented a few failings that I never experienced. At the time, I thought brandishing my weaknesses before peer support groups was assuming a truly humble attitude. But my behavior didn't constitute real regret or real repentance. Actually, I avoided completely turning my will and life over to God's care.

Sayings of the Sages

Behold, I am coming soon! My reward is with me, and I will give to everyone according to what he has done.
     —*Revelation 22:12*

For a while the fool's mischief tastes sweet, sweet as honey. But in the end it turns bitter. And how bitterly he suffers!
     —*Dhammapada, 5*

A Hunk of Healing Humor

If it weren't for Philo T. Farnsworth, inventor of television, we'd still be eating frozen radio dinners.
     —*Johnny Carson*

Daily Affirmation

God is guiding all of my amends making.

Twelve Step Thought

For me, Step Nine wasn't simply or soon carried out. It took months and years of involvement in Twelve Step Programs before I assimilated the spiritual understanding and courage necessary to make appropriate reparations. Yes, I needed a long duration to feel confident in my new way of life. For whatever reasons, I surely was a late bloomer. Yet, once the time was ripe, my behavior demonstrated that I was changing dramatically and positively. Then, it became possible and "safe" for me to speak honestly with persons I had previously hurt. Still, I avoided disclosures that would injure others, or even myself. Mostly, I sought the strength for atoning from my Higher Power.

Sayings of the Sages

The people living in darkness have seen a great light; on those living in the land of the shadow of death a light has dawned.
　　—*Matthew 4:16*

Delivered from passion, fear and anger, absorbed in Me, taking refuge in Me, many purified by the austerity of wisdom, have attained to My state of being.
　　—*Bhagavad Gita IV, 10*

A Hunk of Healing Humor

Now the big thing is Indian roulette. You sit beside a snake charmer with six big cobras—and one of them is deaf.
　　—*Robert Orben*

Daily Affirmation

I seek the strength for atoning from my Higher Power.

Twelve Step Thought

Rather than face the expiation process, had I suspected how weak I really was, I would have reembraced an active addictive state. Or, seeking quicker relief from despair, perhaps I would have committed suicide. Why? Because I've discovered that this rebuilding of overall health and character requires superhuman strength. Now, I know I'm not superhuman. Thus the great emphasis on grace granted by my Higher Power. Only an unlimited Force could possibly permit me to carry out the requisite reconciliation. In order to keep on keeping on, I'm literally forced to turn my life over to the care of an Eternal Entity.

Sayings of the Sages

When a woman who lived a sinful life . . . learned that Jesus was eating at the Pharisee's house, she brought . . . perfume, and as she stood behind him at his feet weeping, she . . . wet his feet with her tears . . . she wiped them with her hair, kissed them and poured perfume on them.
—*Luke 7:37 & 38*

A Hunk of Healing Humor

With me a change of trouble is as good as a vacation.
—*William Lloyd George*

Daily Affirmation

An unlimited Force permits me to carry out reconciliation.

Twelve Step Thought

In pursuing pardon and propitiation with those I have harmed, I humbly ask my Higher Power for the energy and guidance to do the right thing. Once I've done this, I check with others who might be affected, and I consult with my sponsor as well as with my counselor. Then, if a "drastic" move is indicated, I can't afford to back away from it. After all, my preparatory pause was properly productive. My next step is full steam ahead, full throttle toward atonement. I'm ready, H.P. Carry me through the nights of confession and compensation.

Sayings of the Sages

Unless we can realize that we and others are generally behaving as we do because of inculcated biases over which we have no control while we imagine that they are our own opinions, we might do something which would bring about the destruction of all of us. Tolerance . . . has today become a necessity.
—*Idries Shah, Reflections*

A Hunk of Healing Humor

Three may keep a secret if two of them are dead.
—*Benjamin Franklin*

Daily Affirmation

H.P. gives me the energy and guidance to do the right thing.

Twelve Step Thought

In attending to amends, I'm trying to keep in mind that the truth can be used to injure as well as to heal. I've learned the hard way that there is an appropriate approach and moment for telling the truth. Likewise, there's also a time for remaining silent. Even if I were extremely willing to expose the very worst of my wrongs, I'm never justified in buying peace of mind at the expense of other persons. This points up the clear difference between genuine integrity and none at all. My goal is self-honesty as well as being truthful with others. And I look to H.P. for being graced with genuineness.

Sayings of the Sages

If someone wants to sue you and take your tunic, let him have your cloak as well. If someone forces you to go one mile, go with him two miles. Give to the one who asks you, and do not turn away from the one who wants to borrow from you.
  —*Matthew 5:40–42*

A Hunk of Healing Humor

Honesty pays, but it don't seem to pay enough to suit some people.
  —*Kin Hubbard*

Daily Affirmation

My Higher Power is gracing me with genuineness.

Twelve Step Thought

Once I solidly stabilized in recovery, I wanted to leave all my old erroneous ways behind me. I found that I was learning to live in a truly meaningful fashion. Also, I was attempting to compensate for a lifetime of mistakes. In fact, much of my new personal-development program is based on this premise. And time is essential to this propitiation process. After all, my past failures are not the result of chance, and did not occur overnight. I fabricated these messes over a number of years. For perhaps an equal period of time, I'll be rebuilding my life over the ruins of my past. So I seek to transform self-centeredness and the hurt it occasioned for others.

Sayings of the Sages

All things arise from Tao. By Virtue they are nourished, developed, cared for, sheltered, comforted, grown, and protected.
　　—*Tao Te Ching, 51*

Serve God sincerely, and do what is pleasing to him.
　　—*Tobit 13:10*

A Hunk of Healing Humor

I don't care what is written about me so long as it isn't true.
　　—*Dorothy Parker*

Daily Affirmation

My self-centeredness and the hurt it caused others are being transformed.

Twelve Step Thought

Now I'm putting into practice a positive course of conduct that, to some extent, compensates for the hurt my addiction foisted on others. Even so, there may be certain wrongs that I can never significantly right. When such situations present themselves, I'm checking them out with respected peers in recovery. This way I make sure I am not just avoiding unpleasantness. When I can truthfully admit to myself that I would resolve these situations if I ever could, then I need not worry about these uncontrollable points. When I really can't see someone in person, I send an honest letter, followed by a sincere telephone call. Results are up to my Higher Power.

Sayings of the Sages

If God took to himself all men that are in the world . . . and were made man in them, and they were made divine in him, and this work were not fulfilled in me, my fall and my wandering would never be amended except it were fulfilled in me also.

    —*Theologia Germanica, III*

A Hunk of Healing Humor

I wash everything on the gentle cycle. It's much more humane.

    —*Anonymous*

Daily Affirmation

I'm righting all wrongs I can, and not worrying about the rest.

Twelve Step Thought

After putting fair effort into the process of atonement, I was sorely tempted to bypass the more humiliating and feared encounters that remained. Then I realized that, although the approach is much more difficult, I benefit more from going to a former enemy rather than a friend for amends. In such scenarios, I try not to criticize or argue with the persons involved. Rather, I focus on the fact that I'm expressing regret for my hurtful behavior. Placing fearfulness aside, I stride forth, with H.P. at my side, to honestly pursue reconciliation with my former victims.

Sayings of the Sages

Live so that you are at ease, in harmony with the world, and full of joy. Day and night, share the springtime with all things, thus creating the seasons in your own heart.
—*Chuang Tsu: Inner Chapters, 5*

Listen . . . and learn to be wise, and guide your heart in the way.
—*Psalm 23:19*

A Hunk of Healing Humor

It's really hard to be roommates with people if your suitcases are much better than theirs.
—*J. D. Salinger*

Daily Affirmation

With H.P. at my side, I benefit most from going to an enemy for amends.

Twelve Step Thought

Friends in recovery say that I need forgiveness in order to truly recover from my illness. I agree. Yet, for me to accept pardon without returning it would defy all spiritual laws. Something to do with reaping what you sow, I think. And I don't want to threaten my recovering state in any way. Without a doubt, reparation is good for my conscience. Most often, it's also helpful to others. Thus, when someone hurts my feelings or otherwise causes me grief, I will be ready to extend a forgiving hand. All the sages say one should forgive without imposing any limits. Uplifted by my Higher Power, I'm pardoning all who hurt me.

Sayings of the Sages

If you are happy at the expense of another man's happiness, you are forever bound.
　　—*Dhammapada, 21*

If we are distressed, it is for your comfort and salvation; if we are comforted, it is for your comfort, which produces in you patient endurance of the same sufferings we suffer.
　　—*II Corinthians 1:6*

A Hunk of Healing Humor

The brain is a wonderful organ; it starts working the moment you get up in the morning and does not stop until you get to the office.
　　—*Robert Frost*

Daily Affirmation

Today, I'm forgiving others without imposing any limits.

Twelve Step Thought

The satisfaction demanded by Step Nine includes making amends to my body. Physical damage was also one of the ravages of my obsessive illness. Expiation involves having a medical check-up. Proper exercise is further compensation. A wholesome and nutritious diet is de rigeur here. Also, am I tuning in to my excessive oral fixation? Or am I treating my digestive tract like a garbage disposal? When I describe my eating habits, do I engage in rationalization—either minimizing or maximizing what I consume? Do I get enough rest? I need to be disciplined in taking care of my body. H.A.L.T. is essential. I can't be too hungry, angry, lonely, or tired.

Sayings of the Sages

Who is forced to struggle more than he who tries to master himself? This ought to be our purpose, then: to conquer self, to become stronger each day, to advance in virtue.
    —*The Imitation of Christ I, 3*

If a person forgives and makes reconciliation, his reward is due from God.
    —*The Meaning of the Glorious Qur'an XLII, 40*

A Hunk of Healing Humor

Be kind and considerate to others, depending somewhat upon who they are.
    —*Don Herold*

Daily Affirmation

Today, I'm not getting too hungry, angry, lonely, or tired.

Twelve Step Thought

The Twelve Steps comprise one giant amend that I make to God, to other people, and to myself. The Steps form a pattern for properly ordering my life through maximum service to the Divine Beloved and to the persons around me. For me, recovery from the obsession is but a partial amend. It must be followed up by actions that benefit others. In a sense, I effect atonement with the Divinity by looking for its will in all that I undertake. Also, I can best offer satisfaction to my fellow humans by fostering their independence at every opportunity that I get. In all amending, I resort to H.P. through prayer and meditation.

Sayings of the Sages

As he sees the Lord present equally everywhere, he does not injure his true Self by the self and then he attains to the supreme goal.
—*Bhagavad Gita XIII, 28*

Whoever fears the Lord makes true friends, for as a man is, so is his friend.
—*Ecclesiasticus 6:17*

A Hunk of Healing Humor

All progress is based upon the universal innate desire on the part of every organism to live beyond its income.
—*Samuel Butler*

Daily Affirmation

I resort to H.P. through prayer and meditation in all amending.

Twelve Step Thought

Practicing Step Nine is finally putting my life in order. Unknown to me during those years I was sidetracked by obsessive sickness, my true purpose in life has been to prepare myself for serving the Friendly Force and the people I encounter. This is a wholesome objective of the spirit. In this positive sense, I practice atonement through fostering new spiritual habits. Thus, I seek to fully live the Twelve Steps while absorbing what I can of other personal-development systems. In many respects the rest of my life is required for me to complete the Ninth Step. The process of living spiritually is the biggest amend I could ever make.

Sayings of the Sages

When Jesus saw him lying there and learned that he had been in this condition for a long time, he asked him, Do you want to get well?
     —*John 5:6*

Neither may a man who is made a partaker of the divine nature oppress or grieve anyone.
     —*Theologia Germanica, XXXIII*

A Hunk of Healing Humor

No man in the world has more courage than the man who can stop after eating one peanut.
     —*Channing Pollock*

Daily Affirmation

Living spiritually is the biggest amend I can make.

Twelve Step Thought

I've been told by friends in recovery that, if I really work Step Nine, I'll be amazed at the results before I'm halfway through. For starters, my new associates promised that I would no longer regret my past nor want to make it go away. They even affirmed that I would find a new freedom and happiness. They said that I certainly would experience serenity and inner peace. So succulent are the fruits of this principle! That's *if* I do the necessary footwork. I can't harbor any reservations about really living this step, and still expect to remain recovering. Otherwise, my psyche would be too guilt-ridden. H.P., grant me fulfillment.

Sayings of the Sages

Wise men embrace the one and set an example to all. Not putting on a display, they shine forth. Not justifying themselves, they are distinguished.
      —*Tao Te Ching, 22*

A Hunk of Healing Humor

Happiness isn't something you experience; it's something you remember.
      —*Oscar Levant*

Daily Affirmation

I'm finding true freedom and true happiness.

Twelve Step Thought

The promises presaged by my Twelve Step fellows were by no means exaggerated. My life has been very much transformed! My attitude has changed radically in a relatively short time. I'm much less self-centered than I used to be. Even fear has become an infrequent feeling. My old sense of uselessness and self-pity has evolved into a sureness of purpose. I now find myself flowing with situations that earlier would have shattered me. This is indeed the miraculous doorway to the promised land I had been seeking. Following many struggles, the predictions are coming true. A Higher Power is doing for me what I couldn't do for myself.

Sayings of the Sages

The waters of the Jordan separated in front of the ark of the covenant of God, and when it crossed the Jordan, the waters of the river vanished.
    —*Joshua 4:7*

If their purpose or activity is of human origin, it will fail. But if it is from God, you cannot overthrow it.
    —*Acts 5:38 & 39*

A Hunk of Healing Humor

To be good is noble, but to teach others how to be good is nobler—and less trouble.
    —*Mark Twain*

Daily Affirmation

My Higher Power is giving me a sureness of purpose.

Twelve Step Thought

Taking daily inventory and making any necessary adjustments is like flying a passenger jet. The flight-plot computer (Higher Power) alerts the navigational system computer (personal inventory) which arranges appropriate course corrections. A long, smooth flight actually consists of many minor changes in direction. I finally discovered that living is a series of slight realignments. Becoming open to change and becoming ready to be recentered allows me to grow beyond all human expectations.

Sayings of the Sages

He guides me by paths of virtue for the sake of his name.
        —*Psalm 23:3*

See what is. See what is not. Follow the true way.
        —*Dhammapada, 22*

A Hunk of Healing Humor

Ignorance is no excuse—it's the real thing.
        —*Irene Peter*

Daily Affirmation

I am open to the Power that guides me from within.

Twelve Step Thought

Admitting error simply is making a minor course correction. Even knowing this, my obsessional ego still recoils from stating my errors. Me . . . make a mistake! Yet, whenever I admit a blunder with little hesitation, I am rapidly transported to a high state of consciousness. I am more and more living the truth of some early Twelve Step advice: "Hang on to your ass . . . you're in for quite a ride." In fact, amid very mundane activities, I am being rocketed to a new dimension.

Sayings of the Sages

The existence of relative truth does not prove the non-existence of universal truth.
>   —*Idries Shah, Reflections*

The sage is guided by what he feels and not by what he sees.
>   —*Tao Te Ching: Inner Chapters, 12*

A Hunk of Healing Humor

To err is human, but it feels divine.
>   —*Mae West*

Daily Affirmation

Real living comes with constant course corrections.

Twelve Step Thought

"*Continued* to take personal inventory" implies that this principle isn't a short-term matter. Change is a continuing process. So is regular self-assessment, which will be going on for the rest of my life. Yet, knowing this, I'm still committed to live in the *now*. In my case, this self-estimation doesn't necessarily happen on a daily basis. But it's close—perhaps every other day. Wise persons in recovery state that a periodic self-examination is necessary for maintaining and enhancing one's well-being. And, thanks to H.P.'s help, I've gone beyond thinking that I can drop this practice someday. Rather, it has evolved into a booster of my spirituality. Guess I'll be inventorying when I'm ninety-two!

Sayings of the Sages

There is right because of wrong, and wrong because of right. Thus, the sage does not bother with these distinctions but seeks enlightenment from heaven.
—*Chuang Tsu: Inner Chapters, 2*

Stick to the advice your own heart gives you, no one can be truer to you than that.
—*Ecclesiasticus 37:17*

A Hunk of Healing Humor

The trouble with the future is that it usually arrives before we're ready for it.
—*Arnold H. Glasow*

Daily Affirmation

Self-examination is maintaining and enhancing my well-being.

Twelve Step Thought

The nature of profound change is such that my life didn't improve significantly until I made self-searching a regular habit. Before I reached that regularity, I experienced a great deal of struggle, failures, depressing days, hopeless moments. Finally, I hit my emotional bottom; and I surrendered totally to my Higher Power. I asked my spiritual teacher for advice; and I followed the directions given. Miraculously, a regularity of discipline entered my life. Almost daily I performed self-assessment and meditated. Then, I knew that I was undergoing amelioration, a great transformation. Thus, personal inventory, and other practices, contributed to my good fortune.

Sayings of the Sages

Let not a man force a habit upon himself with a perpetual continuance, but with some intermission. For . . . the pause reinforceth the new onset.
   —*Francis Bacon*

Do not lie to each other, since you have taken off your old self . . . and have put on the new self, which is being renewed in knowledge in the image of its Creator.
   —*Colossians 3:9 & 10*

A Hunk of Healing Humor

There is no substitute for incomprehensible good luck.
   —*Lynne Alpern*

Daily Affirmation

Thanks to H.P., I'm undergoing a great transformation.

Twelve Step Thought

I need to admit and accept whatever I discover upon taking personal inventory. Step Ten reminds me that defects such as selfishness, dishonesty, resentment, and fear are problems I'll encounter every day. So I can truly own my condition in this world at any particular time. Whatever failings I discover, I ask Loving Goodness to remove them from me. Also, I set out to do the indicated footwork. I select the most appropriate and available means for patiently and persistently correcting what is wrong. Lately, my experience has been that, when I do my very best, my Higher Power does all the rest. I find that problems are soon resolved.

Sayings of the Sages

The Scripture and the Faith and the Truth say sin is nought else but that the creature turneth away from the unchangeable Good and betaketh itself to the changeable.
—*Theologia Germanica, II*

In your great love, answer me God, faithful in saving power.
—*Psalm 69:13*

A Hunk of Healing Humor

Most people are bothered by those passages of Scripture they do not understand, but the passages that bother me are those I do understand.
—*Mark Twain*

Daily Affirmation

I'm doing my very best; my Higher Power is doing the rest.

Twelve Step Thought

In my mind, the Tenth Step symbolizes a deep desire for self-knowledge and growth. Since I have been led into a vast spiritual dimension, my new goal is to understand this enticing realm and to operate effectively in it. Of the many lessons to be learned, a major one involves being compassionate to others. In fact, loving and tolerating others has become one of my primary objectives. Being in the spirit means that I stop making unreasonable demands of those I love. It also implies that I get in the habit of practicing courtesy and justice with persons I dislike. Enjoying the compassion of my Higher Power prompts me to offer compassion to others.

Sayings of the Sages

I claim that love is built to last forever and your faithfulness founded firmly in the heavens.
    —*Psalm 89:2*

Try to bear patiently with the defects and infirmities of others, whatever they may be, because you also have many a fault which others must endure.
    —*The Imitation of Christ I, 16*

A Hunk of Healing Humor

Kindness is loving people more than they deserve.
    —*Joseph Joubert*

Daily Affirmation

My Higher Power's compassion prompts me to offer compassion to others.

Twelve Step Thought

The phrase "when I was wrong" clearly indicates that I do fall prey to making mistakes. And, when I blunder, I get myself all shook up. A sagacious saying applies here: whenever I'm upset, no matter why, there's something amiss with *me*. Being disturbed is a sign that I misunderstood information that I thought I had grasped. Usually, this occurs when I'm not in a particularly humble frame of mind. Thus, there is no humility as I'm backing away from a discomforting truth into restless mental wanderings. Then my "efforts" to correct my "goofs" merely generate more disturbance for me.

Sayings of the Sages

When Jesus' followers saw what was going to happen, they said, "Lord, should we strike with our swords?" And one of them struck the servant of the high priest, cutting off his right ear. But Jesus answered, "No more of this!"
    —*Luke 22:49-51*

Shall I not drink the cup the Father has given me?
    —*John 18:11*

A Hunk of Healing Humor

I was going to buy a copy of *The Power of Positive Thinking*, and then I thought: What the hell good would that do?
    —*Ronnie Shakes*

Daily Affirmation

I shall drink the cup that my Higher Power is giving me.

Twelve Step Thought

Thinking about the benefits of inventorying brings to mind the immense need for increasing awareness in recovery. Most basically, I've learned that ongoing growth in consciousness is a prime factor in forestalling any possibility of relapse. Happily, whenever I write in my personal journal, I grow ever more aware of my situation. And I'm starting to see the structure that flows through the cycles of my being. In fact, in moments of great moment, I've glimpsed a holistic patterning that *is* my life. Like I'm moving further away from a sleepy, sluggish state toward an intuitive grasping of the very framework of my existence. Now my goals are remaining recovering and becoming closer to H.P.

Sayings of the Sages

An unreflecting mind is a poor roof. Passion, like the rain, floods the house. But if the roof is strong, there is shelter.
> —*Dhammapada, 1*

Is the truly sincere person the one who is trying to save the world or the one trying to save himself from himself?
> —*Vernon Howard*

A Hunk of Healing Humor

To know that we know what we know, and that we do not know what we do not know, that is true knowledge.
> —*Henry David Thoreau*

Daily Affirmation

I'm remaining recovering and becoming closer to my Higher Power.

Twelve Step Thought

There used to be a number of things that I didn't do in a prompt manner. Promptly admitting my errors was a new twist for me. At one time, given my sick sense of inadequacy, my ego couldn't tolerate admitting any mistakes. Forget about owning blunders in a *timely* fashion! I was a great procrastinator. Also, it appears that my honesty was quite selective about its targets. Finally, with the help of a Higher Power, I became able to verbalize my faults. Gradually my admissions took less and less time as I grew more and more honest with myself and others.

Sayings of the Sages

Whatever good happens to thee is from God; but whatever evil happens to thee, is from thy soul.
    —*The Meaning of the Glorious Qur'an IV, 79*

Let us stretch out our hearts and hands to God in heaven. We are the ones who have sinned, who have rebelled.
    —*Lamentations 3:41 & 42*

A Hunk of Healing Humor

One-third of the people of the world are asleep at any given moment. The other two-thirds are awake and probably stirring up trouble somewhere.
    —*Dean Rusk*

Daily Affirmation

Today, I'm readily admitting my errors.

Twelve Step Thought

All the great sages have said that there is a design and a purpose for every creature under heaven. My specific experiences convince me that these wise ones are correct. Reflecting on where I am and on where I've been, I believe there is a reason for my being burdened with addictiveness as well as for my adopting Twelve Step recovery principles. Each person has her or his own dharma or inner law or life pattern which needs to be played out. Now I'm noticing that, the more I'm in sync with my personal pattern, the better my daily existence is. Inspired by the prophetic rays of the stars, I'm painting the perfect self-portrait dreamed up by the Universal Flow.

Sayings of the Sages

Better is one's own law though imperfectly carried out than the law of another carried out perfectly. One does not incur sin when one does the duty ordained by one's own nature.
—*Bhagavad Gita XVIII, 47*

Small is the gate and narrow the road that leads to life, and only a few find it.
—*Matthew 7:14*

A Hunk of Healing Humor

At what other time in history could you find people working night and day to save up enough money to buy labor-saving devices?
—*Robert Orben*

Daily Affirmation

I'm getting in touch with and playing out my own life pattern.

Twelve Step Thought

Once again, as I'm ferried further and further into recovery, I gain an ever-expanding understanding of the relationship among the Twelve Steps. For example, it's clear that three of these principles emphasize the importance of self-examination. At Step Four, I conducted a searching and fearless inventory of my conscience's contents. For the Eighth Step, I listed all the persons that I had hurt, and I became willing to seek atonement with all of them. In practicing Step Ten, I continue to take personal inventory—promptly admitting when I'm in the wrong. And I need H.P. for remaining faithful to this practice.

Sayings of the Sages

A huge area of human life and thought requires the intelligent use of generalizations: which includes using them, modifying them and superseding them.
　　　—Idries Shah, Reflections

You may devote as much time as you wish to causes as long as you don't use them as an excuse for trying to change others instead of yourself.
　　　—Camden Benares, Zen Without Zen Masters

A Hunk of Healing Humor

God cannot alter the past, but historians can.
　　　—Samuel Butler

Daily Affirmation

My Higher Power helps me remain faithful to self-examination.

Twelve Step Thought

Whenever I feel uneasy, I can do an instant inventory. First, I find a quiet place inside myself; then, I look for the problem. Normally, I find that the cause of my discomfort is some imbalance in a basic area of my life. Of course the solution is to get rebalanced. I see this as a spiritual sort of wheel balancing, so that my ride through the day is smoother. Most commonly, I get out of balance due to temporarily forgetting that I have strong addictive tendencies; missing support-group meetings; selfishly not associating with persons new to recovery; and cutting back on my Twelve Step practices. Then, seeking upliftment through a Higher Power, my spirit finds peace again.

Sayings of the Sages

The sage, traveling all day, does not lose sight of his baggage.
—*Tao Te Ching, 26*

Trust wholeheartedly in God, put no faith in your own perception; in every course you take, have him in mind: he will see that your paths are smooth.
—*Proverbs 3:5 & 6*

A Hunk of Healing Humor

When people are free to do as they please, they usually imitate each other.
—*Eric Hoffer*

Daily Affirmation

My Higher Power keeps bringing balance and peace into my life.

Twelve Step Thought

Admitting mistakes and accepting criticism are necessities for me. Trying to justify blunders is so silly! It's really a temper tantrum of my egoistic pride. I have to own the fact that such pridefulness still has a hold on me. I find myself behaving in a self-protective way when there isn't any good reason to do so. I should refuse responsibility for an error because someone will think I'm stupid? Or is it because *I'm* feeling inadequate and dumb? Perhaps someone is simply giving me appropriate input for a possible improvement. Why do I then act so defensively? More than once, I've found myself defending against the nonattack. Time to turn my ego over to the Divine Sustainer!

Sayings of the Sages

[Instant enlightenment] is quite a bit like the overnight success in show business: it's frequently preceded by years of hard work.
—*Camden Benares, Zen Without Zen Masters*

Make sure I do not follow pernicious ways, and guide me in the way that is everlasting.
—*Psalm 139:24*

A Hunk of Healing Humor

He never makes the same mistake twice. Every day he finds some new mistakes to make.
—*Louis A. Safian*

Daily Affirmation

I'm turning my ego over to the Divine Sustainer.

Twelve Step Thought

Paranoia persisted for the longest time as I voyaged into recovery. Why? I don't truly know to this day. Back then, I was quite sure that certain people were out to get me. Naturally, because of my sick beliefs, I gave off negative and suspicious vibrations. In response, some people acted toward me with uncertainty. With my warped perception, I viewed their reactions as justifying my worst fears. They *were* trying to hurt me. What a vicious circle I was caught in! It took me years to get out of it. Thankfully, H.P. relieved me of this insanity. Now I realize I'm the only one who can harm me.

Sayings of the Sages

If you are too flexible and lose your center, then you will be overcome and destroyed. ... If you try to demonstrate your composure, you will be criticized and slandered.
    —*Chuang Tsu: Inner Chapters, 4*

Humble yourselves, therefore, under God's mighty hand. ... Cast all your anxiety on him because he cares for you.
    —*I Peter 5:6 & 7*

A Hunk of Healing Humor

There are very few people who don't become more interesting when they stop talking.
    —*Mary Lowry*

Daily Affirmation

I'm the only one who can hurt me.

Twelve Step Thought

I also do a weekly "shared" inventory. This too constitutes a recommended method for avoiding relapse. When I'm writing in my daily journal, negative feelings held at an unconscious level often bubble up to consciousness. Yet, there still remains a "blind side" to my psychic structure. That's the reason for a once-a-week verbal self-assessment which is related to a person I trust. This sharing provides me with feedback about myself which I might otherwise try to rationalize. I talk with a very close friend for this purpose. Some share with a sponsor. Certain people prefer their therapists. Others employ a fellow Twelve Stepper. The crux of the matter is sharing and trust and increased awareness.

Sayings of the Sages

To take advice of some few friends is ever honourable; for lookers on, many times, see more than gamesters.
    —*Francis Bacon*

Whoever makes thanksgiving his sacrifice honours me; to the upright man I will show how God can save.
    —*Psalm 50:23*

A Hunk of Healing Humor

Don't you know better than to argue with me? If you knew better, you'd know I'm right.
    —*William Roylance*

Daily Affirmation

The crux of verbal self-assessment is sharing, trust, and increased awareness.

Twelve Step Thought

For me, really living is cherishing each moment of the trip. Mostly, review is saved for the evening campsite. Thus, at the end of my day, I can gauge how far I've come. It's best that I limit review to my own inventory. Trying to analyze someone else's motives is a whole other matter, unrelated to my personal progress on the path. When I live in this manner, each moment of each day becomes a lightful opportunity for growth. I refer to this approach as following the way of the heart. When I thus proceed lovingly, I am at one with all creation and its Maker.

Sayings of the Sages

This is the only way, the only way to the opening of the eye. Follow it.
　　　—Dhammapada, 20

The light shines in the darkness, and the darkness has not put it out.
　　　—John 1:5

A Hunk of Healing Humor

Happiness to a dog is what lies on the other side of a door.
　　　—Charleton Ogburn, Jr.

Daily Affirmation

I'm following the path of my heart.

Twelve Step Thought

Although my obsessive sickness has receded into remission, I still can't fancy that I'm fixed forever. Working Step Ten produces an equilibrium that generates the spiritual atmosphere essential to keep growing in recovery. I find there is a triple point of focus involved in so rebalancing myself. I must *think recovered* in order to feel recovered. I must *feel recovered* in order to act recovered. I must *act recovered* in order to be recovering. Part of this process is ongoingly owning my mistakes, and following up with those affected. Then, I can see myself as okay and worthy of future growth. And it's this positive attitude that puts me in the proper emotional, mental, and spiritual condition to continue a strong and serene recovery.

Sayings of the Sages

There will be no more night. They will not need the light of a lamp or the light of the sun, for the Lord God will give them light.
    —*Revelation 22:5*

Flesh gives birth to flesh, and spirit gives birth to spirit.
    —*John 3:6*

A Hunk of Healing Humor

The optimist proclaims that we live in the best of all possible worlds; and the pessimist fears this is true.
    —*James Branch Cabell*

Daily Affirmation

My positive attitude provides me with a strong and serene recovery.

Twelve Step Thought

The most tremendous truths present themselves in very plain wrappings. For example: "If you don't look where you're going, you might run into someone or trip and hurt yourself." That's what the Tenth Step is all about. So simple! Yet, it's not always so easy. For me, it means keeping a personal journal to keep my eyes focused on recovery road. A few persons I know audiotape their reflections about the path, because they cannot relate to writing. This self-searching also involves setting time aside for said review. Most of all, I depend on Divine Goodness for the grace to follow through. I'm powerless otherwise. However, I'm assisted only after completing the requisite footwork.

Sayings of the Sages

As men approach me so do I accept them: men on all sides follow my path.
—*Bhagavad Gita IV, 11*

Blessed be the Lord day after day, the God who saves us and bears our burdens.
—*Psalm 68:19*

A Hunk of Healing Humor

A book is a mirror: If an ass peers into it, you can't expect an apostle to look out.
—*G. C. Lichtenberg*

Daily Affirmation

Upon exercising proper self-estimation, I'm given the grace to follow through.

Twelve Step Thought

Over the years in recovery, I've made some interesting discoveries. For one, not only am I powerless over my obsession, I'm powerless over everything else too. That includes admitting my mistakes to another human being. Not so long ago, I couldn't manage it—especially with those I viewed as "enemies." I even found it difficult to be civil or just be with people who were not on my side. Left to my own devices, I really couldn't relate to persons I disliked. A Power greater than myself had to help me in such situations. First, I had to surrender all claims of being able to handle whatever-it-was. Then, I found myself gifted with calm and deliberate sureness as I proffered apologies.

Sayings of the Sages

When you are quite sure you cannot be brave for yourself, you will attract cosmic bravery.
    —*Vernon Howard*

Have we not expanded thee thy breast and removed from thee thy burden? Verily, with every difficulty there is relief.
    —*The Meaning of the Glorious Qur'an XCIV, 1, 2, 6*

A Hunk of Healing Humor

It is the test of a good religion whether you can joke about it.
    —*G. K. Chesterton*

Daily Affirmation

H.P. gifts me with calm and deliberate sureness in apologizing.

Twelve Step Thought

In my situation, extended emotional upsets can lead to relapse. Anger and resentment especially can keep me in an emotionally edgy state for a long time. Jealousy, self-pity, or wounded pride can do the same thing. An instant inventory, which can be taken at any time of the day or night, assists in soothing such stormy emotions. This on-the-moment assessment is aimed at dealing with the unexpected drastic dips in my days. Actually it's a great method of relapse prevention. It gives me a chance to touch base with H.P. Then, confronting the disagreeableness, I swing into action, and find relief.

Sayings of the Sages

Never act without reflection, and you will have nothing to regret when you have done it.
—*Ecclesiasticus 32:24*

So long as a man clingeth unto the elements and fragments of this world (and above all to himself), and holdeth converse with them, and maketh great account of them, he is deceived and blinded.
—*Theologia Germanica, XIX*

A Hunk of Healing Humor

The worst moment for the atheist is when he is really thankful, and has nobody to thank.
—*Dante Gabriel Rossetti*

Daily Affirmation

I'm taking time for instant inventory and touching base with H.P.

Twelve Step Thought

I also do longer, in-depth self-assessments. This might involve days of recollection or special spiritual retreats. On such occasions, which I have attended annually or even more frequently, I set out to conduct a thorough update of my status. This is the time when I carefully and deliberately review my progress in recovery. Am I growing? For this stock-taking, silence proves golden. In quietness I seriously reflect on where I am and where I'm headed. Perhaps I'll even discover that I wish to change direction in some respect. Certainly, I'll seek frequent conscious contact with my God, and ask for guidance.

Sayings of the Sages

I know not what it is . . . that we spend so much labor and even more anxiety on things that are transitory and mean, while we seldom or never advert with full consciousness to our interior concerns.
— *The Imitation of Christ III, 31*

Jesus often withdrew to lonely places and prayed.
— *Luke 5:16*

A Hunk of Healing Humor

For people who like peace and quiet: a phoneless cord.
— *Unknown*

Daily Affirmation

I'm ever more consciously involved in my interior life.

Twelve Step Thought

Another way of assessing where I am and how I operate is to employ the services of a trained therapist. Such a professional knows how to reach the psychic dungeon where I have placed and forgotten some nasty negative feelings. Better to deal with these when I have the opportunity rather than wait for a searing emotional storm to break out of my unconscious when I least expect it. Being so overwhelmed by emotion would lead me along the road to relapse. Anyway, a really good counselor is like a clean mirror. In this person, I see the reflection of the real me. Feedback helps my awareness grow rapidly. Using therapy's tools, I get the strength to wield them from H.P.

Sayings of the Sages

He who obtains wisdom works his own good, he who cares about discernment finds happiness.
    —*Proverbs 19:8*

He has many followers. ... When he stands up, he does not teach. When he sits down, he utters no word. People go to him empty, and come back full. Is there such a thing as teaching without words?
    —*Chuang Tsu: Inner Chapters, 5*

A Hunk of Healing Humor

The latest thing in psychiatry is group therapy. Instead of couches, they use bunk beds.
    —*Robert Orben*

Daily Affirmation

Feedback helps my awareness grow rapidly.

Twelve Step Thought

Usually toward the end of my day I'm most disposed to reflect on recent events. It has something to do with this being a quieter and less hectic time. Then, my mind isn't so distracted by the outer play of this world. It can gaze inward at the internal record of happenings and at the meaning these hold for me. At times, I feel good about my daily trek. Sometimes, I feel like I cheated myself and others. On occasion, I know I have to apologize for a faux pas. Always, part of this introspective process is renewing my conscious contact with the Loving Divinity.

Sayings of the Sages

Therefore the truly great man dwells on what is real and not what is on the surface, on the fruit and not the flower. Therefore accept the one and reject the other.
—*Tao Te Ching, 38*

A Hunk of Healing Humor

If you look like your passport photo, you're too ill to travel.
—*Will Kommen*

Daily Affirmation

I regularly gaze inward at the meaning life holds for me.

Twelve Step Thought

Self-centeredness lies behind the concerns that appear when I'm working Step Ten. My excessive preoccupation with myself approached narcissism at times. It was like I was wrapped around my own navel. Certainly I had an overblown sense of my personal importance. Now, I'm much more open to others and their needs. Yet, I'm quite fallible. I must proceed with care as I start to attain some degree of status and recognition. I'm positively connected with others today mostly due to the support supplied by the Cosmic Lovingness. Any accomplishments are more Divinity's achievements than mine. Fostering ongoing humility seems to be a basic feature of this step.

Sayings of the Sages

I am going to send you what my Father has promised; but stay in the city until you have been clothed with power from on high.
        —*Luke 24:49*

Vainglorious men are the scorn of wise men, the admiration of fools, the idols of parasites, and the slaves of their own vaunts.
        —*Francis Bacon*

A Hunk of Healing Humor

It's true I'm arrogant, but it's a humble arrogance—not nearly as much as my worth deserves.
        —*William Roylance*

Daily Affirmation

My accomplishments are more Divinity's achievements than mine.

Twelve Step Thought

Over the years, I've heard a number of Twelve Steppers talk about hurts and atonement. From them, I learned there are many ways of making Tenth Step amends. One is to do something nice for people without letting them know that I'm the doer. Another is to radically change my behavior (for the positive) toward someone I wasn't getting along with. Yet another involves treating myself more lovingly rather than trying to carry the crushing weight of perfectionism. No need to be an extremist! Most important is giving of my time, perhaps my most precious possession, to help a suffering fellow human being. Then there's seeking H.P.'s creative inspiration on admitting and correcting wrongs.

Sayings of the Sages

O how sweet it is to enjoy life, living in honesty and strength! And wisdom is sweet, and freedom.
    —*Dhammapada, 23*

Whoever is not against us is for us. I tell you the truth, anyone who gives you a cup of water in my name . . . will certainly not lose his reward.
    —*Mark 9:40 & 41*

A Hunk of Healing Humor

I do not want people to be agreeable, as it saves me the trouble of liking them.
    —*Jane Austen*

Daily Affirmation

H.P. inspires me when I'm admitting and correcting wrongs.

Twelve Step Thought

Life in recovery is all about balance. To see how I'm doing, I tally the events of my day on a fairly regular basis, counting my "shoulds" (basic necessities) and my "wants" (preferences). My needs include such things as the following: eating enough to stay healthy, sleeping, working to pay bills, drinking a minimum of liquids, and other similar functions. My desires would include other items: going to the beach, enjoying ice cream, getting a relaxing massage, visiting a shopping mall, and so forth. For me to remain recovering, there needs to be a better balance between my desires and what I must do for sustained existence. Otherwise, I'm unbalanced and headed for trouble.

Sayings of the Sages

Wisdom and power are His alone. His, to control the procession of times and seasons ... His, to uncover depths and mysteries, to know what lies in darkness; and light dwells with him.
        —*Daniel 2:20-22*

When a man puts away all the desires of his mind ... and when his spirit is content in itself, then he is ... stable in intelligence.
        —*Bhagavad Gita II, 55*

A Hunk of Healing Humor

By the time we've made it, we've had it.
        —*Malcolm Forbes*

Daily Affirmation

I'm gaining a balance between my "wants" and my "shoulds."

Twelve Step Thought

Doing a daily inventory contributes to a gradual but sure increase in awareness. In my growth process, a slight inner realignment follows each small increment in personal development. At any one time, I find that a tiny positive spurt is plenty. The most important element is persistence. All my little efforts finally add up to transformation. Anyway, in my grandiose attempts to force major alterations in my personality I fell flat on my face. The reality of my situation is a seemingly slow spiral upward. Then, I'm ever gaining a higher level and a more panoramic view. Of course, my Higher Power is the motivator behind such constant change.

Sayings of the Sages

The underlying principle of all questioning is that the one who is asked must have the Truth in himself, be able to acquire it by himself.
  —*Sören Kierkegaard*

I know your deeds. See, I have placed before you an open door that no one can shut. I know that you have little strength, yet you have kept my word.
  —*Revelation 3:8*

A Hunk of Healing Humor

I improve on misquotation.
  —*Cary Grant*

Daily Affirmation

I'm becoming transformed through my little daily efforts.

Twelve Step Thought

Until self-restraint becomes an unconscious habit, I'll have trouble subordinating my will to the will of the Divine Self. Without such discipline, I'll find myself jerked around by one impulsive move after another. Whenever an impulse arises, I'm training myself to immediately back away for reflection (behaving appropriately). Also, I analyze honestly just what is involved (thinking appropriately). Then, I check the source of any related emotional earthquake (feeling appropriately). When I'm in the wrong, I admit it; when someone else is in error, I seek to forgive that person. With Goodness's grace, I can profitably practice self-restraint.

Sayings of the Sages

Follow thou the inspiration sent unto thee, and be patient and constant, till God do decide: for He is the best to decide.
    —*The Meaning of the Glorious Qur'an X, 109*

He who loves discipline, loves knowledge; stupid is the man who hates correction.
    —*Proverbs 12:1*

A Hunk of Healing Humor

I consider exercise vulgar. It makes people smell.
    —*Alec Yuill Thornton*

Daily Affirmation

Thank Goodness, I can profitably practice self-restraint.

Twelve Step Thought

To remain recovering, I can't afford to think my obsessiveness has been totally eliminated. Nor can I allow myself to become depressed whenever I start acting out of my addictive mentality. Such instances demand the careful application of behavior modification. Perhaps the most important modifier is the development of self-restraint. This gives me breathing space for reflection. But even with this discipline, I can expect progress, not perfection. A daily reprieve from active obsessiveness constitutes the context of my life. And this relief relies on how well I take care of my spirit. "Caring" is bringing an openness to God's will into all the activities of my day.

Sayings of the Sages

The intrusion of the doctrine of "the older the better" is a characteristic of the irrationality which must break out somewhere in people who are trying too hard to be rational.
—*Idries Shah, Reflections*

Just to see how we endlessly repeat our self-damaging behavior is a small but definite light along the path.
—*Vernon Howard*

A Hunk of Healing Humor

The two hardest things to handle in life are failure and success.
—*Anonymous*

Daily Affirmation

I expect progress today, not perfection.

Twelve Step Thought

Over time, I've started to see how all persons are subject to some degree of emotional illness and to making mistakes. Human nature is fallible. That's reason enough for my having compassion for others and for myself. There's really no point in my being angry at or hurt by people who are very much like myself. We all suffer somehow from the growing pains of life! Feelings like pride, resentment, and related negative ego "stuff" constitute emotional quicksand that I can't chance walking on. In fact, I can't effectively put aside my obsessiveness unless I assume a recovery posture that is humble, honest, compassionate, and in touch with a Higher Power.

Sayings of the Sages

Until God ordains otherwise, a man ought to bear patiently whatever he cannot correct in himself and others.
—*The Imitation of Christ I, 16*

God restored Job's fortunes, because he had prayed for his friends. More than that, God gave him double what he had before.
—*Job 42:10*

A Hunk of Healing Humor

The only normal people are the ones you don't know very well.
—*Joe Ancis*

Daily Affirmation

Today, I have compassion for others and for myself.

Twelve Step Thought

Whenever I do an inventory, I'm able to visualize how I'll do better. Before recovery, I had never achieved accurate self-appraisal. Now, taking stock, on occasion the wholeness of my life flashes before my eyes. A complete matrix of meaning—connecting all the cycles and patterns of my being—instantaneously fills my mind. For the shortest second, I grasp all the interrelationships of existence. Recovery is holistic. Downplaying any major practice impacts on all the others. When I carefully follow the Twelve Steps, I sense my soul swiftly being suffused with the Divine Spirit. And this consciousness of the Supreme puts me into a higher state.

Sayings of the Sages

The perfect accept the law along with such ignorant men as understand and know nothing better ... that they may be restrained thereby, and kept from evil ways, or if it be possible, brought to something higher.
　　—*Theologia Germanica, XXVI*

I have endowed him with my spirit.
　　—*Isaiah 42:1*

A Hunk of Healing Humor

Laugh and the world laughs with you, snore and you sleep alone.
　　— *Anthony Burgess*

Daily Affirmation

Following the Twelve Steps puts me into a higher state.

Twelve Step Thought

It took me a while to realize that I had already experienced contacts with God at many levels. When I became absorbed in watching waves rolling relentlessly toward the shore, I was gripped by the divine flux. When I melted into and flowed with my favorite music, I became attuned to celestial melodies. When I lost myself in the eyes of my beloved at the orgasmic height of loving, I felt the throb of Ultimate Energy. And now I look forward to enhancing this conscious contact.

Sayings of the Sages

Amend your behavior and your actions, and I will stay with you.
>   —*Jeremiah 7:3*

The master guards his watching. It is his most precious treasure.
>   —*Dhammapada, 2*

A Hunk of Healing Humor

You have to stay awake to make your dreams come true.
>   —*Anonymous*

Daily Affirmation

Today I am in touch with my Higher Power.

Twelve Step Thought

Prayer and meditation are scintillating crystals that capture my attention. Prismlike, these ancient and proven methods truly focus light within. And, when my within is lit up, I more easily "see" a divine presence. Just in seeking to improve my conscious contact, It sometimes envelops me in a radiance of Spiritfire. What a blessing! This meditative approach becomes a laser-beam that fills the facets of my crystalline spirit and that focuses my mind on my Greater Self.

Sayings of the Sages

In what measure we put off the creature, in the same measure are we able to put on the Creator.
— *Theologia Germanica, I*

Having fixed the mind on the Self, let him not think of anything else.
— *Bhagavad Gita VI, 25*

The sage has no mind of his own.
— *Tao Te Ching, 49*

A Hunk of Healing Humor

The little I know, I owe to my ignorance.
— *Sacha Guitry*

Daily Affirmation

My attention is focused on my Greater Self.

Twelve Step Thought
Meditation has become the magical ingredient in the improvement of my conscious contact with the Cosmic Source. And I'm not downplaying the importance of prayer, which broadens the conduit to the Eternal Sustainer. But for me, contemplation is even more crucial in deepening the channel to the Divine. Meditating literally fills my soul with spiritual gold. At one point, it was a discipline I sorely needed. Over time, it has evolved into a serenity generator that I seek out as much as possible. It's an openness to the Loving Divinity, which constitutes the fullness of my humanity. Guided by H.P., when I meditate, I touch the wholeness of a new way of life.

Sayings of the Sages
Store up for yourselves treasures in heaven, where moth and rust do not destroy, and where thieves do not break in and steal. For where your treasure is, there your heart will be also.
    —*Matthew 6:20 & 21*

It is our fullest "humanhood," the fullest use of what it means to be human, that is the goal of meditation.
    —*Lawrence Le Shan*

A Hunk of Healing Humor
Platitudes are the Sundays of stupidity.
    —*Anonymous*

Daily Affirmation
Meditation supports my new way of life.

Twelve Step Thought

Upon detaching myself from any thoughts rambling around my mind, I can reach the point of high receptivity in meditation. Somehow, a connection with Divinity occurs. God graces me with supernatural vision. I begin to "see" in a much different manner than usual. Then, I'm being blessed with a transcendent view of my reality. When I look at the universe, everything seems transformed. The whole world appears glowing with a bright yet soft white light, tinged quite subtly with blue or violet. Once or twice, when my spirit has "turned" to gaze at the Sublime One, I have "felt" that I shared the infinite power of the divine.

Sayings of the Sages

Thou cannot behold Me with this [human] eye of yours; I will bestow on thee the supernatural eye. Behold My divine power.
    —Bhagavad Gita XI, 8

The Eye with which I see God is the same Eye with which God sees me.
    —Meister Eckhart

A Hunk of Healing Humor

Men are born with two eyes, but only one tongue, in order that they should see twice as much as they say.
    —Charles Caleb Colton

Daily Affirmation

I'm being blessed with a transcendent view of my reality.

Twelve Step Thought

Prayer is a superhighway connecting me with Infinite Spirit. On awakening, I open my day by reverently turning my attention to the One who sustains me. This devotion constitutes the preparatory phase of launching another daily adventure. Therein, I ask the Cosmic Guide to direct my thinking for the following twenty-four hours. Also, throughout my day's journey, I pause periodically for recontacting the Eternal Energy. At such moments, I often repeat, "Your will, not mine, be done." These refreshing spirit breaks are especially important when I feel stressed out or in great doubt about what to do. Before going to sleep, I thank the Beloved for all the blessings bestowed on me today.

Sayings of the Sages

If a man were to do thus [enter the mind of God] a thousand times a day, each time a fresh and real union would take place; and in this sweet and divine work standeth the truest and fullest union that may be in this present.

—*Theologia Germanica, VIII*

A Hunk of Healing Humor

Pray: to ask that the laws of the universe be annulled in behalf of a single petitioner confessedly unworthy.

—*Ambrose Bierce*

Daily Affirmation

Prayer connects me with Infinite Spirit.

Twelve Step Thought

The "sought" of Step Eleven's "sought through prayer and meditation" is based on two universal principles. The first: *seek and you shall find*. The second: *as you seek, so shall you find*. When I was honestly seeking a Higher Power, mercifully it allowed itself to be found. Though I am the needy seeker, the Divine Beloved does want us to be together. Also, when I came from a very emotionally charged and selfish place, the result of my search was a snakepit of negative feelings, ever in painful flux. When I aim for spiritual goals first and foremost, I get everything else I need too. If I make spiritual goals the single sun around which I move, then I'm taken care of today.

Sayings of the Sages

Seek first His kingdom and his righteousness, and all these things shall be given to you as well. Therefore do not worry about tomorrow, for tomorrow will worry about itself.
    —*Matthew 6:33 & 34*

When the lower earnestly seeks the higher, the higher allows itself to be found.
    —*Vernon Howard*

A Hunk of Healing Humor

It is better to know some of the questions than all of the answers.
    —*James Thurber*

Daily Affirmation

I'm aiming for spiritual goals first and foremost.

Twelve Step Thought

Sometimes it's extremely difficult either to meditate or to pray. When I'm in that situation, my inner landscape feels barren, dry, and downright depressing. Then, I must resort to an emergency appeal for assistance from the grace-bestowing Power. The Serenity Prayer constitutes one such safety valve: "God, grant me the serenity to accept the things I cannot change, courage to change the things I can, and wisdom to know the difference." This request for divine intercession can be repeated as often as necessary. Also, focused on faith, I keep telling myself that my Inner Guide will get me through the day.

Sayings of the Sages

God, I am calling, hurry to me, listen to me, I am invoking you. My prayers rise like incense.
    —*Psalm 141: 1 & 2*

It is good for us to have trials and troubles at times, for they often remind us that we are on probation and ought not to hope in any worldly thing.
    —*The Imitation of Christ I, 12*

A Hunk of Healing Humor

God sends meat and the devil sends cooks.
    —*Thomas Deloney*

Daily Affirmation

My Inner Guide will get me through the day.

Twelve Step Thought

Repeating a particular prayer throughout a difficult day proves very calming for me. It gives me a better chance of regaining my balance. The repeated use of a prayerful phrase was referred to as *japa* by some of the ancient sages. To help focus the mind on this praying, they used a rosary (or *mala*) of wooden beads or seeds. This was called a bead roll, or "telling" one's beads, or saying of the rosary. The Eastern Orthodox "Jesus Prayer" is one such calmative. A special name of God (or *mantra*) is another. Yet another is the "Hail Mary." And, as this orison becomes synchronized with the inbreath and the outbreath, I flow into the holy breathing of the Universal Flow.

Sayings of the Sages

If we live in the Spirit, let us also walk in the Spirit.
    —*Galatians 5:25*

His joy and anger flow like changing seasons. He is in harmony with all things and has no limitations.
    —*Chuang Tsu: Inner Chapters, 6*

A Hunk of Healing Humor

California is the only state in the union where you can fall asleep under a rose bush in full bloom and freeze to death.
    —*W. C. Fields*

Daily Affirmation

Repeating the name of God is my calmative.

Twelve Step Thought

While I was wrapped around my own obsessiveness, I talked a good line about how I was seeking Ultimate Reality. But, really, I sought the chimera that possessed my soul. I was like a constantly operating machine, about to break down, with an unreachable "off" switch. Yet, deep down, I longed to be released. As the psychological computer ran wild, my program finally crashed. It was too painful to restart the same program. I surrendered. Then came Twelve Step programming. Then, the possibility and desirability of becoming close to a sympathetic Divinity. At last I sought heartfully the enhancement of that special connection.

Sayings of the Sages

You will keep him in perfect peace, whose mind is stayed on You, because he trusts in You.
    —*Isaiah 26:3*

This world is in darkness. How few have eyes to see! How few the birds who escape the net and fly to heaven!
    —*Dhammapada, 13*

A Hunk of Healing Humor

When something good happens it's a miracle and you should wonder what God is saving up for you later.
    —*Marshall Brickman*

Daily Affirmation

I'm seeking my special connection with the Divine.

Twelve Step Thought

When I practice meditation regularly, I open myself to receiving intuitive messages from the Inner Self. This is when the still, small voice within speaks words of encouragement to the ear of my soul. Going within is the route to serenity for my spirit. Despite numerous and varied attempts, I never found peace "out there." The kingdom of God isn't visible to the outer eye. For me, it is in the meditative state that a profound and very real union with the Divine takes place. And my personal growth goal is attaining constant contact with Eternal Spirit.

Sayings of the Sages

The kingdom of God does not come visibly, nor will people say, "Here it is," or "There it is," because the kingdom of God is within you.

—*Luke 17:20 & 21*

I will instruct you and teach you in the way you should go.

—*Psalm 32:8*

A Hunk of Healing Humor

I have a prodigious quantity of mind; it takes me as much as a week sometimes to make it up.

—*Mark Twain*

Daily Affirmation

Going within is my route to serenity.

Twelve Step Thought

Talking about "improving" my conscious contact implies that it continues to get better. Like an onion, progress is a process with a number of phases that get peeled away one by one. I'm admitting to some spiritual advancement rather than to established supernatural wholeness. God knows how much of a trek I still have to go! Yet, my life definitely has improved. Not so long ago, any connection I had with the Divine was mostly unconscious. At this point, I'm in a much better place. I made peace with myself, with people I had hurt, and with God. As I grow ever more in touch with this Higher Power, I become increasingly serene. Within, I stroll through Allah's peaceful garden.

Sayings of the Sages

God doth call to the Home of Peace: He doth guide whom He pleaseth to a Way that is straight. To those who do right is a goodly [reward] . . . they are Companions of the Garden.
—*The Meaning of the Glorious Qur'an X, 25 & 26*

A Hunk of Healing Humor

Why is it that we rejoice at a birth and grieve at a funeral? It is because we are not the person involved.
—*Mark Twain*

Daily Affirmation

I'm more serene as I'm more in touch with my Higher Power.

Twelve Step Thought

There is a wise saying in Twelve Step Programs: "Be careful what you pray for; you might just get it." In other words, my prayers are answered, but not necessarily in the way that I expect. There's an apocryphal story about a man who prayed to lose thirty pounds fast. The next day, consequent to a terrible accident, his right leg was permanently severed. He did indeed lose thirty pounds fast! In praying, when I come from a selfish place, when I insist on a certain response time, when I claim to know the perfect solution, I'm setting myself up for getting a nasty surprise from the Universe. Maybe I'll leave it up to H.P.

Sayings of the Sages

Other men are sharp and clever, but I alone am dull and stupid. Oh, I drift like the waves of the sea, without direction, like the restless wind. Everyone else is busy, but I alone am aimless ... I am different. I am nourished by the great mother.
    —*Tao Te Ching, 20*

I can do everything though him who gives me strength.
    —*Philippians 4:13*

A Hunk of Healing Humor

The only reason some people get lost in thought is because it's unfamiliar territory.
    —*Paul Fix*

Daily Affirmation

The response to any of my prayers is up to my Higher Power.

Twelve Step Thought

That expression "God as we understood Him" is open-ended. Over the years in recovery, my conception of the Divinity has changed quite radically. I no longer consider the Divine Entity as a "He." I see such gender references as a spin-off of a patriarchal social system. In my book, the Eternal Good is sexless. The more accurate pronoun is "It." The old anthropomorphic picturing of the Supreme Sustainer has died for me. Rather, I view "It" as Cosmic Consciousness, as the Conscious Being without limits—in which beingness I am somehow a participant. Thankfully, I've found a spiritual program that doesn't impose a particular form of deity on me!

Sayings of the Sages

And God said to Moses, "I Am who I Am."
    —*Exodus 3:14*

Allow the inner instructor to guide you toward the inner treasure.
    —*Vernon Howard*

A Hunk of Healing Humor

Most of my friends are not Christians, but I have some who are Anglicans or Roman Catholics.
    —*Dame Rose Macaulay*

Daily Affirmation

The inner Instructor is guiding me toward inner treasure.

Twelve Step Thought

How can a human being understand a god anyway? My mind has been staging that debate for quite a while. From the grace that I've received so far, I can conclude only that there is an immanent reality which is greater than my little self. Each of us is free to define this Ultimate however we want. But strangely enough, both the physicists and the mystics seem to be approaching agreement on this question. David Bohm, a distinguished physicist and perhaps Einstein's greatest student, defines ultimate reality as a *nonmaterial substratum out of which everything emerges*. What could such a "nonmaterial" Energy Source possibly be? And why is it that, when I turn inside for meditation, I find myself energized?

Sayings of the Sages

Depth in philosophy bringeth men's minds about to religion: For while the mind of man looketh upon second causes scattered ... when it beholdeth the chain of them ... it must needs fly to Providence and Deity.
    —*Francis Bacon*

A Hunk of Healing Humor

A pious man is one who would be an atheist if the king were.
    —*Jean de La Bruyére*

Daily Affirmations

I'm given grace by an immanent reality greater than my little self.

Twelve Step Thought

For many years, I found myself far removed from praying for knowledge of a Higher Power's will for me. My stubborn self-centeredness blocked the way. When I finally did get down to some sincere and serious prayer, what I asked for first was peace of mind. I sought relief from the terrible psychic pain that had terrorized my life so completely. So my initial petitions to the Divinity were still selfish. It was only when I started to understand the need for selfless service that I began seeking to be free from self-will. No longer could I settle for making requests, which were mostly for me. At last, I truly sought to know the Supreme Being's will for me.

Sayings of the Sages

The spirit of a man is the lamp of the Lord, searching all the inner depths of his heart.
    —*Proverbs 20:27*

How curious that people should be more interested in the charge that I am "against God," than in the question whether God is against me.
    —*Idries Shah, Reflections*

A Hunk of Healing Humor

A fanatic is a man who does what he thinks the Lord would do if He knew the facts of the case.
    —*Finley Peter Dunne*

Daily Affirmation

I'm seeking the Supreme Being's will for me.

Twelve Step Thought

My best friend in the whole world once taught me a wonderful lesson about following the divine design. Like many other persons in recovery, I often wondered how I would recognize what the Force intended for me. After all, the ways of the Eternal One are mysterious for mere mortals like myself. How could I possibly determine that a particular course of action I selected was responding to the desire of the Divine? One day, as my friend and I chatted about this matter, she gave me the answer that I needed: whatever happens to me *is* God's will. Wow! What a revelation! Until then, I couldn't have conceived of such a simple solution. Yet, what I had believed before was okay. It's just that I was ready for more.

Sayings of the Sages

Ye shall not will except as God wills, the Cherisher of the Worlds.
—*The Meaning of the Glorious Qur'an LXXXI, 29*

Listen to My supreme word, the most secret of all. Well beloved art thou of Me, therefore I shall tell thee what is good for thee.
—*Bhagavad Gita XVIII, 64*

A Hunk of Healing Humor

This free-will business is a bit terrifying anyway. It's almost pleasanter to obey, and make the most of it.
—*Ugo Betti*

Daily Affirmation

God is telling me what is good for me.

Twelve Step Thought

The phrase "and the power to carry that out" implies that both knowing and doing divine will are dependent on grace, on a Higher Power. I know this is true because my experience is that I'm powerless over everything. I don't have enough strength to appropriately handle difficult situations on my own. So I turn to the Powerful Sustainer for help. Going it all alone would be mistaking recovery for cure. As it is now, I'm feeling a lot of gratitude for the gift of recovering one day at a time. I need the Spiritual Sun's light to walk on my path. I need the glow of God's inspiration, the infusion of Its energy, and the consciousness of Its contact.

Sayings of the Sages

Lord, you yourself light my lamp, my God lights up my darkness.
　　—Psalm 18:28

Walk while you have the light, before darkness over-takes you. Put your trust in the light while you have it, so that you may become sons of light.
　　—John 12:35 & 36

A Hunk of Healing Humor

Wouldn't it be funny if we fought our next war over disarmament?
　　—Robert Orben

Daily Affirmation

The Spiritual Sun's light allows me to walk on my path.

Twelve Step Thought

A FANTASY ON CONSCIOUS CONTACT
AND ACCEPTANCE

On the side of a cliff I clung to a stumproot starting to fray. Uncertainty was promised as soon as I heard the wood splitting. Powerless to resolve this dilemma, paradoxically I remained as calm as if my mother cradled me in her arms. Spying a luscious raspberry within my reach, I plucked it ever so gently; and, placing it in my mouth, I savored this small, tart-sweet gift. Then, when the tiny stump gave way, I trustingly accepted God's call to another place.

Sayings of the Sages

After me will come one who is more powerful than I, whose sandals I am not fit to carry. He will baptize you with the Holy Spirit and with fire.
    —*Matthew 3:11*

Peace I leave with you; my peace I give to you. . . . Do not let your hearts be troubled and do not be afraid.
    —*John 14:27*

A Hunk of Healing Humor

I am not absent-minded. It is the presence of mind that makes me unaware of everything else.
    —*G. K. Chesterton*

Daily Affirmation

Today, I'm accepting God's call.

Twelve Step Thought

Improvement in my conscious contact with Divinity doesn't deny my inherently human characteristics. In other words, I don't stop being me because I'm more in touch with Loving Consciousness. I still must get sufficient rest, eat enough nutritious food, exercise my body on a regular basis, and associate with some like-minded peers. I also need to be honest, to be real. I need to be in touch with the unique person I am. I like to joke around. I'm heavy on philosophy, comparative religion, creative writing, and rehabilitation. I enjoy walking in the woods, responding to the spontaneity of children, smiling at the spirit sparkling in people's eyes.

Sayings of the Sages

When we are awake, our senses open. We get involved with our activities and our minds are distracted.
    —Chuang Tsu: Inner Chapters, 2

Do you eat sensibly? . . . Do you have sensible sleeping habits? . . . Do you get plenty of fresh air, sunshine, exercise and contact with nature?
    —Peace Pilgrim

A Hunk of Healing Humor

Most people who give up smoking take up a substitute: irritability!
    —David de Chiron

Daily Affirmation

In seeking God, I'm not denying my humanity.

Twelve Step Thought

From my perspective, prayer and meditation are also *as I understand them*. Prayer is positive self-talk, sprinkled throughout my day. Meditating is very simply emptying my mind of distracting thoughts. This getting in touch with God is a highly personal venture. Therefore, no one can tell others *exactly* how to pray or how to meditate! There are a number of suggested methods for both. Most important are the sincerity and the regularity of these two practices. For either, how can I use someone else's method perfectly when I'm a totally different person? Anyway, the proof is in the pudding. Constructive thinking does connect me with the Universal Flow. And focusing my consciousness increases my serenity.

Sayings of the Sages

Never be completely unoccupied, but read or write or pray or meditate or do something for the common good.
  —*The Imitation of Christ I, 19*

Could you not keep watch [meditate] for one hour? Watch and pray so that you will not fall into temptation. The spirit is willing, but the body is weak.
  —*Mark 14:37 & 38*

A Hunk of Healing Humor

How can one conceive of a one-party system in a country that has over two hundred varieties of cheese?
  —*Charles de Gaulle*

Daily Affirmation

I'm praying and meditating daily with great sincerity.

Twelve Step Thought

In all areas of my life, there's a beneficial practicality in contemplation and divine petition. Meditation and prayer take care of soul serenity. Recreation relaxes the body towards physical peacefulness. As my conscious contact with God increases, I more frequently reach emotional balance. At times, I am amazed at my mental composure in the midst of trying circumstances. As I work on bettering my godly connection, both my personal life and my professional life take a turn for the better. When I maintain the status of a seeker, the Universe gives me whatever I need.

Sayings of the Sages

You need to meditate daily. If you learn letting go in meditation, then that will permeate your personal life and your professional life also.
    —*A yogic friend*

Believe, meditate, see. Be harmless, be blameless. Awake to the law. And from all sorrow free yourself.
    —*Dhammapada, 10*

A Hunk of Healing Humor

Happiness is having a large, loving, caring, close-knit family in another city.
    —*George Burns*

Daily Affirmation

When I remain a seeker, the Universe gives me what I need.

Twelve Step Thought

My ongoing recovery hinges on staying in solid spiritual shape. On the other hand, enhancing my spiritual awakening depends on further change, i.e., positive growth in my personality. To accomplish these seemingly paradoxical tasks, I must ignore my negative ego's claim to power. Thus, I place my trust totally in a Power much greater than myself. My Higher Power has already demonstrated miracles in my life. So I feel that I can count on additional assistance whenever I need it. Somehow, I intuitively "know" that a Supreme Being lovingly watches over me. I'm confident that, when I turn to the Source of Grace, all will be well for me.

Sayings of the Sages

You should pray to God ... and just let go of your feelings of negativity.
　　　—Nityanandaji

Real Virtue seems unreal ... great talents ripen late; the highest notes are hard to hear; the greatest form has no shape. The Tao is hidden and without name. The Tao alone nourishes and brings everything to fulfillment.
　　　—Tao Te Ching, 41

A Hunk of Healing Humor

We have two kinds of morality side by side: one which we preach but do not practice, and the other which we practice but seldom preach.
　　　—Bertrand Russell

Daily Affirmation

All is well for me when I turn to the Source of Grace.

Twelve Step Thought

Meditation is like stepping from the cold darkness (of self) into the warm and comforting Spiritual Sunlight (of Self). My soul too needs its own light to grow. After years of trying meditation, I found a deepening of the experience. Deep meditation is a quiet mind empty of the footfalls of flitting thoughts. Some sages say that, when I meditate on my spiritual teacher or on God, I become like them. What a happy thought! When the subliminal self makes a connection, I'm instantaneously transformed. This spiritually-energized focus allows me to "gaze" into the fullness of the Godhead. On occasion, I've even glimpsed the radiant reality of the Divine Being.

Sayings of the Sages

One comes to be like what one meditates on. If you think continually of sin, you will become a sinner. . . . If you worship God, you become God.
        —*Baba*

To be able to look into eternity whenever he will. . . . A single one of these excellent glances is better, worthier, higher and more pleasing to God, than all that the creature can perform as a creature.
        —*Theologia Germanica, VIII*

A Hunk of Healing Humor

There are two kinds of light—the glow that illumines . . . and the glare that obscures.
        —*James Thurber*

Daily Affirmation

As I meditate on Spiritual Sunlight, I become more lightful.

Twelve Step Thought

Meditative contact graces me with a sure sense of belonging. In this mode, whenever I catch a glimpse of the divine will, the seeming craziness around me no longer deeply disturbs me. When I'm on the same universal frequency, I find myself truly in tune with the Holy Spirit's wishes for me. I want to know the Supreme One's intentions for me; meditating is a sturdy doorway into God's will. Often, I end my morning meditation with a supplication that H.P. keep showing me my next move. Over time, I find that my connection with Divinity is improving. I usually add "if it is your will" to my requests. What God wants *is* the crux of life.

Sayings of the Sages

I am not alone. I stand with the Father who sent me.
    —*John 8:16*

Everyone who has left houses or brothers or sisters or father or mother or children or fields for my sake will receive a hundred times as much and will inherit eternal life.
    —*Matthew 19:29*

A Hunk of Healing Humor

"If Today Were a Fish, I'd Throw It Back In."
    —*Song title*

Daily Affirmation

My connection with Divinity is improving.

Twelve Step Thought

I used to wonder mightily about the meaning of this world of ours. But lately in meditation, Eternal Energy is hinting to me that this universe is a giant stage and that all of us are actors; Shakespeare was right. I resisted the notion before because I was still taking life *very seriously*. Actually, I was quite confused by the strange twists that my meditative meanderings were taking. How could I possibly follow a trail which seemed to dead-end in an all-encompassing cosmic joke? Why was I now smiling when I overheard someone talking about getting ahead in life? Ahead of whom or what? Can it be that Supreme Being blissfully amuses itself with a vast play of consciousness?

Sayings of the Sages

When a man hath thus broken loose from ... all temporal things and creatures, he may afterwards become perfect in a life of contemplation.
—*Theologia Germanica, XII*

Everything is the pervasion of the supreme truth. God has created the play of the world for his own pleasure. The world is just a play, an entertaining movie. It is neither true nor false.
—*Bhagawan Nityananda*

A Hunk of Healing Humor

The only way to amuse some people is to slip and fall on an icy pavement.
—*Ed Howe*

Daily Affirmation

Today, I can laugh and see everything as permeated by Supreme Truth.

Twelve Step Thought

When relating to others is involved, Step Eleven returns me to the powerlessness of the First Step. Not only do I not control my own life, but I also don't control the lives of others. In like manner, just as I pray that the divine intention be done for myself, so too do I pray that God's will be done for others. Also, it's when I forget myself that I truly find myself. When I'm asleep to the things of this world, then I'm wide awake to eternal life. Now I'm into turning others over to *their* Higher Powers. Superfixer I'm not! And I find the strength to resist this role in daily meditation and prayer.

Sayings of the Sages

Balance is the perfect state of still water. Let that be our model. It remains quiet within and is not disturbed on the surface. . . . Because virtue has no outward form, nothing can escape from it.
  —*Chuang Tsu: Inner Chapters, 5,*

Never accept the confused or unpleasant behavior of other people as your problem, for it is theirs alone.
  —*Vernon Howard*

A Hunk of Healing Humor

Hope is the feeling you have that the feeling you have isn't permanent.
  —*Jean Kerr*

Daily Affirmation

I'm turning others over to their Higher Powers.

Twelve Step Thought

Maybe I need to improve my conscious contact with *all* beings. If I have any psychic connection with the Divinity, so do persons I encounter. Is the Sublime One any less with them than with me? Thinking otherwise, especially with my poor track record of approaching the Unapproachable, would be merely a judgment by my negative ego. Therefore, it behooves me to have a respectful attitude toward my fellow human beings. I can consistently remind myself that the God who dwells in me also resides in every other person and in all things. So it's important that I act respectfully toward all people and toward all the creation of the Almighty Creator.

Sayings of the Sages

Keep on loving each other as brothers. Do not forget to be hospitable to strangers, for by so doing some people have entertained angels without knowing it. Remember those in prison as if you were their fellow prisoners, and those who are mistreated as if you were being mistreated.
    —*Hebrews 13:1-3*

A Hunk of Healing Humor

All celebrated people lose dignity on a close view.
    —*Napoleon Bonaparte*

Daily Affirmation

Today, I'm acting respectfully toward all people and all creatures.

Twelve Step Thought

When I let go of my growth practices to any serious extent, I really feel it in my life. I find myself in a very "dry" and uncomfortable place. As I look back, I realize that my feelings, my mind, and my spirit have been deprived of some essential support. This is true whenever I don't regularly inventory my personal-development status. It also happens when I neglect prayerful praise and contemplation. Just as my body can become debilitated due to insufficient nourishment, so too can my psyche and soul be malnourished. I need open channels to the Source of Grace. It's become evident to me that prayer and meditation are my main methods of consciously connecting with Divine Consciousness.

Sayings of the Sages

If you cannot recollect yourself continuously, do so once a day at least. . . . In the morning make a resolution and in the evening examine yourself on what you have said this day, what you have done and thought.
    —*The Imitation of Christ I, 19*

The Lord is my rock and my fortress and my deliverer; my God, my strength, in whom I will trust.
    —*Psalm 18:2*

A Hunk of Healing Humor

There is nothing in the world so enjoyable as a thorough-going monomania.
    —*Agnes Repplier*

Daily Affirmation

Prayer and meditation are my main methods of connecting with Divine Consciousness.

Twelve Step Thought

Even though I truly don't understand the Supreme Being, I do want to improve the conscious connection between us. Over time, the response I've received to my prayers has produced inner peace much beyond my earlier expectations. After years of enhancing my entry to a meditative state, I now often get lost in the depths of meditation. For a brief while, my little "i" goes away; and the big "I Am" of the Holy Spirit (or Shakti or Tao or Cosmic Energy) comes in. Or is it that, when I let go, I'm letting God hold it together? Perhaps the Ultimate Good was always within me, and my ego just got out of the way.

Sayings of the Sages

Meditation is the vigorous search for the true identity of the "me," not a psychic jugglery nor a technique for deep relaxation.
  —*Venkatesananda*

I will sing to the Lord as long as I live; I will sing praise to my God while I have my being. May my meditation be sweet to Him; I will be glad in the Lord.
  —*Psalm 104:33 & 34*

A Hunk of Healing Humor

Take egotism out, and you would castrate the benefactor.
  —*Ralph Waldo Emerson*

Daily Affirmation

When I let go, I'm letting God hold it together.

Twelve Step Thought

I've been informed by fellow seekers that inventory and prayer and meditation are necessary preparations for well-founded Twelve Step work. When I pray properly, I become more harmonized with the Universe's Law of Being. When I meditate effectively, I glimpse the pattern of Consciousness forming a unity that is miraculous. In fact, I'm then tripping into the dimension of Spirit. My invocation is to be aware of what God intends for me as well as for the strength to do the related footwork. Also, practicing meditation daily helps me maintain my connectedness with a Loving Power greater than myself. And all this preparing led me to a spiritual awakening.

Sayings of the Sages

There will be pain in your spiritual growth until you will to do God's will and no longer need to be pushed into it. When you are out of harmony with God's will, problems come—their purpose is to push you into harmony.
    —*Peace Pilgrim*

This is my commandment: love each other as I have loved you.
    —*John 15:12*

A Hunk of Healing Humor

We are all here on earth to help others; what on earth the others are here for I don't know.
    —*W. H. Auden*

Daily Affirmation

Practicing meditation daily helps me maintain my connection with H.P.

Twelve Step Thought

My ongoing spiritual awakening has been like an ever-growing fire raging deep within me. As I continue to pursue Twelve Step practices, some fiery angel seems to stand by—periodically stoking my inner conflagration into white-hot incandescence. And the burning strips away dark stains disfiguring my character. Already these pride-devouring flames are transforming my ego—paradoxically passing from searing heat into soothing coolness.

Sayings of the Sages

The wretched, however, he saves by their very wretchedness, and uses distress to open their eyes.
    —*Job 36:15*

To him who overcomes, I will give the right to eat from the tree of life, which is in the paradise of God.
    —*Revelation 2:7*

A Hunk of Healing Humor

May you live all the days of your life.
    —*Jonathan Swift*

Daily Affirmation

Any glitches in my day are just the cleansing flames.

Twelve Step Thought

The self-help group sages say that if you practice all eleven prior principles to the best of your ability, you will have a spiritual awakening. They didn't claim that it would be a one-time, instantaneous explosion of ecstasy. In my case at least, there were no flashing lights or ringing bells or angels blowing heavenly trumpets. Rather, my coming out of soulsleep has happened at varying intervals and with different intensities. Yet, there is absolutely no question in my mind that I have experienced a bona fide spiritual awakening. Also, I'm not alone. There are others with me on the path of personal development. Somehow, that thought consoles me when the soulful spiral upward seems agonizingly slow.

Sayings of the Sages

God is spirit, and his worshipers must worship in spirit and in truth.
    —*John 4:24*

I felt a complete willingness to dedicate my life to service. I tell you, it's a point of no return. After that, you can never go back to completely self-centered living.
    —*Peace Pilgrim*

Hunk of Healing Humor

A little inaccuracy sometimes saves tons of explanation.
    —*H. H. Munro*

Daily Affirmation

I'm dedicating my life to service.

Twelve Step Thought

I remember my initial spiritual awakening quite vividly. Motivated by a sincere love, I had just agreed to render service to some fellows in recovery. Still feeling that loving spirit, I started to speak at a meeting when it came my turn to share. Abruptly, I was wrapping up my words. And I felt *very* different! I glanced at my watch. I had been talking for twenty minutes, but I couldn't remember anything I had said! Usually, I deliberately decided what to say. Suddenly, it dawned on me that I had spoken spontaneously from my heart for the first time in recovery! When I experienced loving others sincerely, I became open to the transforming love of a Higher Power.

Sayings of the Sages

We have known and have believed the love that God has for us. God is love. Whoever lives in love lives in God, and God in him.
  —*I John 4:16*

This love so maketh a man one with God, that he can never more be separated from Him.
  —*Theologia Germanica, XLI*

A Hunk of Healing Humor

I've always been interested in people, but I've never liked them.
  —*W. Somerset Maugham*

Daily Affirmation

When I live in love, I live in God.

Twelve Step Thought

A spiritual awakening is like starting all over again from an entirely different perspective. There is a prayer that pertains to this transforming: "Tire not of new beginnings: build thy life, never on regret, always upon resolve! Shed no tear on the blotted page of the past, but turn the leaf—and smile—to see the clean white page before thee." It's quite true. From what I've learned, many have found a whole new life in recovery. There are days in recovery when I've turned a page, and marveled at the untouched lifespace before me. So, once again, I pass from the slumbering night of complacency to a day full of promise.

Sayings of the Sages

I am engaged in a great undertaking.
   —*Nehemiah 6:3*

Do You, the Lord my God, everlasting truth, speak lest I die and prove barren if I am merely given outward advice and am not inflamed within; lest the word heard and not kept, known and not loved, believed and not obeyed, rise up in judgment against me.
   —*The Imitation of Christ III, 2*

A Hunk of Healing Humor

Sleeping is no mean art. For its sake one must stay awake all day.
   —*Friedrich Nietzsche*

Daily Affirmation

I'm passing into a day full of promise.

Twelve Step Thought

As a result of practicing these Steps, I have experienced something called a spiritual awakening. Being so renewed is a grace that I receive from my Higher Power. Each time the miracle occurs, I'm gifted with a new state of consciousness and being. The person who looks back is never the same as the individual who was back there. In fact, whenever I'm lifted to a higher plateau, I'm being transformed in more ways than one. As a result, I've secured a source of strength many times greater than a thousand suns combined. I've stepped into a world of spirit, serene beyond my wildest expectations.

Sayings of the Sages

I tell you the truth, whatever you did for one of the least of these brothers of mine, you did for me.
    —*Matthew 25:40*

Nowadays men shun mercy, but try to be brave; they abandon economy, but try to be generous; they do not believe in humility, but always try to be first. This is certain death.
    —*Tao Te Ching, 67*

A Hunk of Healing Humor

Eternal rest sounds comforting in the pulpit; well, you try it once, and see how heavy time will hang on your hands.
    —*Mark Twain*

Daily Affirmation

I've secured a great source of strength and serenity.

Twelve Step Thought

Sometimes it seems that I'm totally engulfed by darkness. At such moments, the things in my life all appear to be going downhill. Then, I can get quite depressed. I try to isolate myself from other persons. I tend to neglect my personal-growth practices. Yet, even though I occasionally get stuck in night, I've finally learned that the dawn *always* comes. There *never* fails to be a light at the end of an apparently endless tunnel. Perhaps there always was a lamp on the front of my miner's hat, needing only my finger to flick the "on" switch. Even better, there's a Power greater than myself guiding me through the dark.

Sayings of the Sages

God, Truth, Reality does not want you to be scared of anything, which is why it requests your earnest attention to the healing messages.

—*Vernon Howard*

Why so downcast, my soul, why do you sigh within me? Put your hope in God: I shall praise him yet, my saviour, my God.

—*Psalm 42:5*

A Hunk of Healing Humor

God Almighty never created a man half as wise as he looks.

—*Thomas Carlyle*

Daily Affirmation

There's a Higher Power guiding me when it's dark.

Twelve Step Thought

When I leave the realm of darkness, I enter the kingdom of luminosity. From the deep and lurid sleep of Death, I pass into the lustrous and vibrant awakening of Life. Then, I'm proceeding on a path that really seems to be taking me somewhere. And I've been placed on this heartful highway by my Higher Power. This is where the prior recovery principles—especially Steps Two, Three, Seven, and Eleven—connect with the Twelfth Step. As my inner glow increases, I can humbly recognize the Source of my growth. True, I must increase in willingness. However, without grace, my noonday sparkle dims to mundane murkiness.

Sayings of the Sages

Talent is the presence of ability and absence of understanding about the source and operation of knowledge.
　　—*Idries Shah, Reflections*

Blessed and holy are those who have part in the first resurrection. The second death has no power over them, but they will be priests of God.
　　—*Revelation 20:6*

A Hunk of Healing Humor

Death is a very dull, dreary affair, and my advice to you is to have nothing whatever to do with it.
　　—*W. Somerset Maugham*

Daily Affirmation

Thanks to my Higher Power, my inner glow is increasing.

Twelve Step Thought

For another phase of my spiritual awakening, I was sitting at an evening meeting; sometime during various people's sharings, the whole scene shifted without warning. The quality of the light in the room palpably changed to a golden hue. Everything "softened" in my line of vision. It seemed like I could see individual chunks of air or light. Also, those who were talking faded into the distance—as if someone had turned the volume way down. Their voices, though less distinct, became more pleasant to my ear. I felt surrounded by an invisible web of serenity. My soul crossed another threshold then.

Sayings of the Sages

Only he who has transcended sees this oneness. He has no use for differences and dwells in the constant. To be constant is to be useful. To be useful is to realize one's true nature. Realization of one's true nature is happiness.
    —*Chuang Tsu: Inner Chapters, 2*

You too are gods, sons of the Most High, all of you.
    —*Psalm 82:6*

A Hunk of Healing Humor

Be careful about reading health books. You may die of a misprint.
    —*Mark Twain*

Daily Affirmation

I'm surrounded by an invisible web of serenity.

Twelve Step Thought

An old-timer on the path gave me this advice: if you faithfully follow the directions of your Inner Guide, you'll soon be living in a reborn and wonderful world. How true! As I practiced personal-growth principles ever more in depth, I realized that my whole being was gradually being transformed. And I had to listen in a totally one-pointed manner so that I would hear the soundless words of my Higher Power, telling me what I should do. When I pay attention to this guidance from within, then my inner world becomes tranquil and serene even if a storm is raging around me. Seeking awareness is a further phase of my spiritual awakening.

Sayings of the Sages

And to thy Lord turn (all) thy attention.
    —*The Meaning of the Glorious Qur'an XCIV, 8*

What dwelleth here I know not, but my heart's full of love and the tears trickle down.
    —*Eleventh-century Japanese poem*

A Hunk of Healing Humor

For those of you interested in reducing your bills, it's simple. Put them on microfilm.
    —*Robert Orben*

Daily Affirmation

I'm ever more open to following the directions of my Inner Guide.

Twelve Step Thought

Without a doubt, the Twelve Steps serve as stepping stones to highly significant psychic advancement. In my own case, tremendous positive changes occurred after I redid Steps Four, Five, Eight, and Nine. The year following these renewals turned into a period of incredible personal growth. Any real results happened over time. Such a seemingly cruel word: time! Yet, the years involved in my spiritual awakening have produced a profound personality transformation for the better. Now I'm a lot more accepting of human foibles—including my own. And I've developed a lot clearer and much more individual understanding of the Divine Being.

Sayings of the Sages

Your work is to discover your work and then with all your heart to give yourself to it.
    —*Dhammapada, 12*

To be afraid of men is a snare, he who puts his trust in the Lord is secure. Many a man seeks a ruler's favour, but the rights of each come from the Lord.
    —*Proverbs 29:25 & 26*

A Hunk of Healing Humor

It is difficult to get a man to understand something when his salary depends upon his not understanding it.
    —*Upton Sinclair*

Daily Affirmation

H.P. helps me continue my spiritual transformation.

Twelve Step Thought

Years into recovery, I realized that some people I knew were relapsing because the Steps alone weren't enough for them. They were sincere. They attended lots of self-help meetings. They talked with their sponsors. And they worked the Steps to the best of their ability. Yet, they "slipped." But why? In further investigating relapse, I learned that a barrier of negative feelings (or behavior patterns) that have been repressed or located at an unconscious level can prevent the full practice of Twelve Step principles. And you can't avoid obstacles that you can't see. Fortunately, these friends sought competent therapists who helped them discover and cope with their obstacles. Then, they could thoroughly follow the path.

Sayings of the Sages

[Too great tasks] will make him dejected by often failings. . . . At the first, let him practice with helps, as swimmers do with bladders or rushes.
—*Francis Bacon*

Let us stop passing judgment on one another. Instead, make up your mind not to put any stumbling block or obstacle in your brother's way.
—*Romans 14:13*

A Hunk of Healing Humor

I don't jog. If I die I want to be sick.
—*Abe Lemons*

Daily Affirmation

I'm seeking all the help I need to thoroughly follow the path.

Twelve Step Thought

In my own way, I've been trying to carry a message of hope to others. There is a way that leads to true peace of mind, to serenity of the spirit, to accepting one's role in this zany universe. Of course, walking this soulpath requires a disciplined self. Yes, here's another anxiety-producing word: discipline! Yet the very disciplining of my self paradoxically and proportionately increases my level of freedom. I'm gradually being liberated from confining programs entered into my computer years ago. The good news that I bring to others is this: a day at a time, liberation is entirely possible.

Sayings of the Sages

He who teaches this supreme secret to My devotees, showing the highest devotion to Me, shall doubtless come to me.

—*Bhagavad Gita XVIII, 68*

I have given them the glory that you gave me, that they may be one as we are one. . . . You sent me and have loved them even as you have loved me.

—*John 17: 22 & 23*

A Hunk of Healing Humor

I am strongly in favor of common sense, common honesty, and common decency. This makes me forever ineligible for any public office.

—*H. L. Mencken*

Daily Affirmation

A day at a time, I'm being liberated by H.P.

Twelve Step Thought

My growth formula tells me to carry the message, not the obsessive person. Thus, I'm properly helping others to help themselves. Knowing where I came from, whenever possible, I bring the good news of recovery to those who still suffer. Perhaps a ray of hope is sowed in their souls. And, in this endeavor, I can cooperate with professionals, because my only purpose is to be helpful. Passing on the knowledge of how to live a renewed life while recovering is also an essential activity for maintaining my own recovering status. Yet, as I'm not carrying the persons, how these individuals react is entirely their decision. I can extend a hand; they must clasp it.

Sayings of the Sages

Never think of any right effort as being fruitless—*all* right effort bears good fruit, whether we see results or not.
>   —*Peace Pilgrim*

As for your intention, who could have learnt it, had you not granted Wisdom and sent your holy spirit from above? Thus, have the paths of those on earth been straightened.
>   —*Wisdom 9:17 & 18*

A Hunk of Healing Humor

We are all worms, but I do believe that I am a glow worm.
>   —*Winston Churchill*

Daily Affirmation

Passing on a ray of hope helps maintain my recovery.

Twelve Step Thought

Even as a relative newcomer, I obtained much personal benefit in trying to help a fellow seeker who was more blind than I. Somehow too, I didn't expect this individual to love me in return or say thank you. There is a divine paradox involved in carrying the recovery message, as I receive my own reward in the act of giving. Just as I liberally received assistance from my teachers, I can freely help others to transcend the "unfairness" of life. Surrounded by my fellows, I both give and get the sort of loving that doesn't demand anything in return. In fact, I find that, when I either participate in or speak at Twelve Step meetings, I'm carrying a message of unconditional love. And upholding my involvement is Eternal Energy.

Sayings of the Sages

The sage never tries to store things up. The more he does for others, the more he has. The more he gives to others, the greater his abundance.
　　—Tao Te Ching, 81

All the believers were one in heart and mind.
　　—Acts 4:32

A Hunk of Healing Humor

Income tax returns are the most imaginative fiction being written today.
　　—Herman Wouk

Daily Affirmation

Eternal Energy supports me in freely helping others.

Twelve Step Thought

When I return love for anger, I carry the message. When I learn from my detractors, I carry the message. When I reply to seeming blame with warmth instead of sarcasm, I carry the message. When I respect people's right to be rather than seek control, I carry the message. When I follow the flow rather than fight the current, I carry the message. When I share my story with another obsessive-compulsive personality, I carry the message. Then again, in my transformed perception, the message carries me.

Sayings of the Sages

What good is it ... if a man claims to have faith but has no deeds?
—*James 2:14*

That which is free, none may call his own ... in the whole realm of freedom, nothing is so free as the will.
—*Theologia Germanica, LI*

A Hunk of Healing Humor

Great talkers are little doers.
—*Benjamin Franklin*

Daily Affirmation

Easy does it, but do it.

Twelve Step Thought

In addition to practicing growth principles, the message of recovery is to focus on twenty-four-hour-a-day living. By applying these guidelines in my daily life, I gain emotional balance. On a one-day-at-a-time basis, I more readily experience the joy of living, which is the keynote of Step Twelve. This is vital information which I can share with others. Yet, I must remember that true knowledge and understanding derive from a Loving Divinity. I must resist the temptation to become the almighty director of newcomers. I'm not the world authority on any topic. I must keep in mind that inappropriate advice could cause someone more trouble than she or he had before. Still, service is recognizing a debt of gratitude to my Higher Power.

Sayings of the Sages

Who scoffs at his neighbor is a fool; the man of discernment holds his tongue.
    —*Proverbs 11:12*

Always remember your end [goal] and do not forget that lost time never returns.
    —*The Imitation of Christ I, 25*

A Hunk of Healing Humor

There is so much good in the worst of us and so much bad in the best of us that it's hard to tell which of us ought to reform the rest of us.
    —*Ogden Nash*

Daily Affirmation

I'm gaining emotional balance by applying the Steps today.

Twelve Step Thought

Later on in recovery, I attended a weekend spiritual retreat. By the end of the first day, I wasn't particularly impressed. When my turn to share came, I honestly admitted that I felt neutral. The next morning there was a long meditation session. While meditating, I got lost in some deep state. Then, a sweet melody was being chanted as participants left the room. Suddenly, my whole being was shaken, filled with strange but blissful meaning. Joyous tears streamed down my cheeks. My heart flipped inside out within me. When I "came to," the room was empty. (Later, I learned that someone had shaken me three times to no avail.) My neutrality had vanished! Feeling so connected to the Divine, I exploded into this phase of spiritual awakening.

Sayings of the Sages

Then the angels showed me the river of the water of life, as clear as crystal, flowing from the throne of God.
      —*Revelation 22:1*

His radiance came from his inner light.
      —*Chuang Tsu: Inner Chapters, 6*

A Hunk of Healing Humor

"Good" has many meanings . . . if a man were to shoot his grandmother at a range of 500 yards, I should call him a good shot, but not *necessarily* a good man.
      —*G. K. Chesterton*

Daily Affirmation

Today, I'm feeling connected to the Divine.

Twelve Step Thought

Sharing one's own spiritual trip with fellow travelers on the path is a potent method of carrying the message. Through analogy, we can all participate in the good news of possible personal transformation. When I listen to others tell their stories, I identify with their highs and their lows. I recognize moments when Divine Grace carried them. I note how they dealt with painful events in their lives. And I draw whatever lessons I feel are applicable to me from the recital of their life events. Also, the fact that we're gathered together, seeking a greater balance in our lives, mysteriously pervades the room with Cosmic Consciousness. Synergistic sharing enhances the serenity of all assembled!

Sayings of the Sages

Where two or three are assembled in my name, there am I with them.
    —*Matthew 18:20*

And verily he will find the roots of the good and the bad, the fruitful and the fruitless, all entwined together in the silent heart of the earth.
    —*Kahlil Gibran*

A Hunk of Healing Humor

There is nothing so absurd but some philosopher has said it.
    —*Cicero*

Daily Affirmation

Sharing sincerely with fellow seekers enhances my serenity.

Twelve Step Thought

Serving as a sponsor or spiritual director or teacher is yet another avenue for bringing the message of recovery to others. In sponsoring a newcomer or a more experienced seeker, both the other person and myself must be intent on walking a day at a time in the path of spiritual progress. In fulfilling this role appropriately, I draw upon the experience of those who trod this way before me. And, although I avoid carrying the person, I cannot withhold reasonable assistance without endangering my own daily respite from obsession. It's not my giving that is a matter of consideration, but when and how I give. So I count on the guidance of my Higher Power for proper sponsorship.

Sayings of the Sages

First take the plank out of your own eye, and then you will see clearly to remove the speck from your brother's eye.
    —*Matthew 7:5*

People who speak or act in an ordinary fashion are most likely to be those who have been the recipients of higher experiences.
    —*Idries Shah, Reflections*

A Hunk of Healing Humor

Experience is the name so many people give to their mistakes.
    —*Oscar Wilde*

Daily Affirmation

I count on the guidance of my Higher Power for proper sponsorship.

Twelve Step Thought

I can best carry the message by the example of my own life. A positive highlight of my personal growth program is frequent contact with newcomers and with other recovering people. I can engage in soul-expanding conversations with them before and after self-help meetings. However, if someone doesn't desire to change her or his behavior, I need not waste time on fruitless persuasion. If such persons believe another route to recovery is possible, I merely encourage them to follow the dictates of conscience. At the most fundamental level, I can share with others my obvious belief in being guided and supported by my Higher Power.

Sayings of the Sages

Anything done in charity, be it ever so ... trivial, is entirely fruitful inasmuch as God weighs the love with which a man acts rather than the deed itself.
  —*The Imitation of Christ I, 15*

For such He has written Faith in their hearts, and strengthened them with a spirit from Himself.
  —*The Meaning of the Glorious Qur'an LVIII, 22*

A Hunk of Healing Humor

God ... is always on the side which has the best football coach.
  —*Heywood Brown*

Daily Affirmation

I best carry the message by the example of my own life.

Twelve Step Thought

Practice is the price of proficiency for me. In order to fully grow my soul, I try to practice these principles in all my doings. Most of all, I work at being in God's presence. I try to live as if I really believe in a Power greater than my self. The thrust of my life is built on spiritual guidelines. I've found that faith, to be truly living, needs to be expressed in the context of self-sacrifice and generous actions toward others. At the same time, I can't worry about what others think of me. I seek to base all my activities on the directions from my Inner Guide. What counts is how I think of and support other seekers. In all this, my Higher Power graces me with the necessary strength.

Sayings of the Sages

Do not merely listen to the word, and so deceive yourselves. Do what it says.
     —James 1:22

What others think about you is never as important as what you think about them.
     —William Wilson

A Hunk of Healing Humor

The difference between genius and stupidity is that genius has its limits.
     —Anonymous

Daily Affirmation

I'm serving others according to the directions of my Inner Guide.

Twelve Step Thought

I've found that "two-stepping" simply doesn't cut it in recovery. I need to practice all twelve principles in all my activities; only admitting my powerlessness and working with active addicts isn't enough. From what I've observed, it's also very difficult for others to direct their destinies using just part of Step One and part of Step Twelve. Personal growth demands much more effort and self-discipline. All the Steps relate to total truthfulness. I must really focus on communicating honestly with others *and* with myself. Steps Two through Ten are important for actually *living* my life. Finally, I recognize that the strength to work the Steps comes from H.P.

Sayings of the Sages

Let your servants see what you can do for them, let their children see your glory. May the sweetness of the Lord be on us! Make all we do succeed.
　　—*Psalm 90:16 & 17*

Flee unto Him for shelter with all thy being. . . . By His grace shalt thou obtain supreme peace and eternal abode.
　　—*Bhagavad Gita XVIII, 62*

A Hunk of Healing Humor

If you want a place in the sun, prepare to put up with a few blisters.
　　—*Abigail Van Buren*

Daily Affirmation

Thanks to H.P., I'm being honest with myself and others.

Twelve Step Thought

Now comes the tough part: exemplifying in my own life what I readily recommend to my fellow seekers. Once again, I recognize and accept that to walk the way I talk takes a lot of self-discipline. Ouch! There's that painful word again: discipline. Yet, I *am* capable of acting honestly when I am surrounded by falseness. When some negativity or badness struts about, I can still proceed from my own positive values. And, when hate is directed at me, I nevertheless can respond in a loving fashion. In fact, I'm told that those who are seriously seeking self-realization form a fellowship or a circle of love. May the Source of Love guide my steps on this path!

Sayings of the Sages

As I have loved you, so you must love one another. All men will know that you are my disciples if you love one another.
    —*John 13:34 & 35*

This is the way of peace: Overcome evil with good, falsehood with truth, and hatred with love.
    —*Peace Pilgrim*

A Hunk of Healing Humor

The reason lightning doesn't strike twice in the same place is that the same place isn't there the second time.
    —*Willie Tyler*

Daily Affirmation

Today, I'm doing that which I recommend to others.

Twelve Step Thought

Whenever I'm stuck in a selfish mode, I tend to force
issues instead of going with the flow and learning to
serve others. Negative ego gets in my way. It's impossible to practice the Steps in all areas of my life while
I'm still trying to arrange the world my way. Yet, after
years of recovery, I'm coming closer to giving up
battling anybody or anything. Also, when feasible, I'm
ready to assist fellows in recovery. And I'm now willing
to turn my troubles into a practical demonstration of
faith. An example would be meeting financial obligations that arise unexpectedly, resigning myself to the
divine will. My Higher Power will keep me moving on
the path.

Sayings of the Sages

Happiness or sorrow—whatever befalls you, walk on
untouched, unattached.
    —*Dhammapada, 6*

It is easier for a camel to go through the eye of a needle
than for a rich man to enter the kingdom of God.
    —*Matthew 19:24*

A Hunk of Healing Humor

There are many scapegoats for our sins, but the most
popular is providence.
    —*Mark Twain*

Daily Affirmation

H.P. keeps me moving on the path.

Twelve Step Thought

These days, it seems that holidays (they used to be "holy days," a time of spiritual renewal) have degenerated into shopping orgies. In recovery, I've faced the fact that acquisition fantasies and materialistic bingeing can only end with the ultimate purge, death. Also, at this time of year, there is often a frenetic pursuit of a fabled holiday spirit. The expectation level for how happy we are supposed to feel can be tough to contend with. Such an emotionally charged atmosphere weighs heavily on those of us with significant addictive traits. Why should I care more or express my caring more for people at certain times of the year while less at other times? My goal is to pursue an ongoing holiday spirit one day at a time.

Sayings of the Sages

Nature likes to have some external comfort in which it can take . . . delight, but grace seeks consolation only in God, to find her delight in the highest Good, above all visible things.
—*The Imitation of Christ III, 54*

Blessed are the dead who die in the Lord . . . they will rest from their labor, for their deeds will follow them.
—*Revelation 14:13*

A Hunk of Healing Humor

A study of economics usually reveals that the best time to buy anything is last year.
—*Marty Allen*

Daily Affirmation

This is a time of spiritual renewal for me.

Twelve Step Thought

According to the sages, serving others is a divinely ordained mission. The path to perfection involves service. Whatever their condition, one's fellow human beings are to be loved for God's sake. The Loving Divinity makes no distinctions for benefiting mankind. Rain falls on the crops of the unjust as well as on those of the just. Food is most often made available to the sinner as well as to the saint. How can *I* pretend to know a better behavior than that of the Eternal One? Even the holiest, like Jesus, hung out with "low" people: fishermen, prostitutes, tax collectors, lepers, and satanists. So my attitude is changing; I don't see anyone as a failure.

Sayings of the Sages

The sage takes care of all men and abandons no one. He takes care of all things and abandons nothing.
    —*Tao Te Ching, 37*

It is useless and wrong to try to help people who want your attention but not your help.
    —*Vernon Howard*

A Hunk of Healing Humor

Except during the nine months before he draws his first breath, no man manages his affairs as well as a tree does.
    —*George Bernard Shaw*

Daily Affirmation

Today, I'm serving others for God's sake.

Twelve Step Thought

I've intuited from my Inner Guide that I'll be increasingly involved in passing out food (of a spiritual sort) to those who are still starving. Perhaps I can exhibit empathy, as I've suffered great starvation in my soul. At times, I felt there was a vast hole in the middle of my being. The emptiness of my heart produced immense hurt. Anomie is agony! However, as soon as I turned to a Higher Power for meaningful assistance, my existential crater began to fill with the light of Eternal Energy. Now, at the very least, I can let those who are ready know that such foodstuffs are available. Fortunately, this supply will never run out.

Sayings of the Sages

I have food to eat that you know nothing about. My food is to do the will of the one who sent me.
—*John 4:32 & 34*

When they had finished eating, Jesus said to Simon Peter, "Simon, son of John, do you truly love me more than these?" . . . "Feed my lambs."
—*John 21:15*

A Hunk of Healing Humor

Part of the secret of success in life is to eat what you like and let the food fight it out inside.
—*Mark Twain*

Daily Affirmation

The supply of spiritual food will never run out.

Twelve Step Thought

How can I possibly see anyone as a failure when I have barely begun to experience some measure of success in life through the Twelve Steps? The positive thrust of my present existence is based on practicing these principles to the best of my ability. As long as an unknown obstacle doesn't prevent me from fully working the Steps, a personal transformation is inevitable. In the final analysis, achieving such results is a gift of grace from my Higher Power. In fact, the more that I admit my little self is powerless, the more strength seems to flow into my life. It appears that, somehow, I'm divinely anointed for (or dedicated to) playing an ever more involved role in helping others.

Sayings of the Sages

How God anointed Jesus of Nazareth with the Holy Spirit and power, and how he went around doing good and healing all who were under the power of the devil, because God was with him.

    —Acts 10:38

To receive God's commands and his counsel and all his teaching, is the privilege of the inward man, after that he is united with God.

    —Theologia Germanica, XXXIX

A Hunk of Healing Humor

What this country needs is more unemployed politicians.

    —Edward Langley

Daily Affirmation

Any results achieved are a gift from my Higher Power.

Twelve Step Thought

Without being melodramatic, I simply have accepted the fact that my body will die someday. And I don't know when. Hey, that's reality! All the more justification for living to the fullest today. All the more reason for seeking a right dependence on the Supreme Being, relieving myself of victim attitudes and unreasonable fears. Concentrating on monetary values and on achieving financial independence cannot take priority over developing the relationship with my Higher Power. I need and want my existence to be useful and serene. If I'm beset by fearfulness, then living is meaningless regardless of my financial condition. Right belief and right action are the keys to the good life.

Sayings of the Sages

As the baggage is to an army, so is riches to virtue. It cannot be spared, nor left behind, but it hindreth the march.
    —*Francis Bacon*

The man who with his whole heart serves God will be accepted, his petitions will carry to where God dwells.
    —*Ecclesiasticus 35:20*

A Hunk of Healing Humor

People ought to start dead and then they would be honest so much earlier.
    —*Mark Twain*

Daily Affirmation

I'm living my life to the fullest today.

Twelve Step Thought

The winding down of the calendar year provides me with an opportunity for reviewing my personal-development journal. So, I can reflect on the significant events in my life over the last twelve months of days. Did I meet the daily challenge of life's lesser, but more ongoing problems? Sure, I called on Providence for the seeming catastrophes. But did I turn to the Divine in other instances too? If not, my reaction needs to be pursuit of further spiritual growth. Have I appropriately been dependent on Ultimate Love rather than on other persons or on things? The absolute bottom line is this: my recovery and self-realization depend on the quality of my relationship with my Higher Power.

Sayings of the Sages

Through devotion he comes to know Me, what My measure is and who I am in truth; then, having known Me in truth, he forthwith enters into Me.
    —*Bhagavad Gita XVIII, 55*

Accept your positive experiences without taking credit and you have humility. Accept your negative experiences without blame and you have serenity.
    —*Camden Benares*

A Hunk of Healing Humor

For every ten jokes, thou has got an hundred enemies.
    —*Laurence Sterne*

Daily Affirmation

H.P. is helping me reflect on the events of the past year.

Twelve Step Thought

The sages say that the end is not the end. Thus, what I think of as finality is really a new beginning. What follows an ending or a death is actually a rebirth or a resurrection. Even more, the wise ones proclaim that we are Spirit, that Spirit was never born and cannot die. Hard stuff to grasp! Yet, it strikes a note in my heart. Anyway, it appears that my present calling is to be wherever I can be of most help to others. By staying on the firing line of life with loving motivation and courage, the Divine Sustainer will shield me from all harm. I place all my trust in H.P., and give this legacy to newcomers and old-timers alike: Think of what you can give instead of what you can get.

Sayings of the Sages

The mind of a perfect man is like a mirror. It grasps nothing. It expects nothing. It reflects but does not hold. Therefore, the perfect man can act without effort.
   —*Chuang Tsu: Inner Chapters, 7*

I tell you the truth, unless a man is born from on high, he cannot see the kingdom of God.
   —*John 3:3*

A Hunk of Healing Humor

A man does not have to be an angel in order to be a saint.
   —*Albert Schweitzer*

Daily Affirmation

Graced by H.P., I'm thinking of what I can give to others.

David Rioux, M.Ed., C.A.C., C.A.S., is Director of Research, Development, and Education at College Hill Medical Center, East Stroudsburg, Pennsylvania. His educational background includes a masters in rehabilitation from Northeastern University and a B.A. in philosophy with counseling and theology coursework from Oblate College and Seminary. David has held faculty appointments at Sussex County (NJ) Community College, Edmonds (WA) Community College, and at Chapman College (CA). He also served as a Trustee of the San Diego Coalition on Alcohol Problems. At College Hill, he has developed the clinical programming for three innovative treatment tracks: a free-standing dually-diagnosed (psych/addiction) unit, a 21-day adolescent program, and a 14- to 21-day multi-modal relapse program. David holds membership in the American College of Addiction Treatment Administrators and is published in the *Student Assistance Journal*, *AAOP Journal*, the *Journal of Psychoactive Drugs*, and the *Journal of Substance Abuse Treatment*. He has been a presenter at numerous workshops and conventions.